Perspectives on welfare

Introducing Social Policy

Series Editor: David Gladstone

Published titles

Perspectives on Welfare
Alan Deacon

Risk, Social Policy and Welfare
Hazel Kemshall

Comparative Social Policy: Theory and Research
Patricia Kennett

Education in a Post-welfare Society
Sally Tomlinson

Perspectives on welfare

Ideas, ideologies and
policy debates

ALAN DEACON

Open University Press
Buckingham • Philadelphia

Open University Press
Celtic Court
22 Ballmoor
Buckingham
MK18 1XW

email: enquiries@openup.co.uk
world wide web: www.openup.co.uk

and
325 Chestnut Street
Philadelphia, PA 19106, USA

First Published 2002

A catalogue record of this book is available from the British Library

ISBN 0 335 20320 5 (pb)   0 335 20321 3 (hb)

Library of Congress Cataloging-in-Publication Data
Deacon, Alan
    Perspectives on welfare: ideas, ideologies, and policy debates/Alan Deacon.
        p. cm. – (Introducing social policy)
    Includes bibliographical references and index.
    ISBN 0-335-20321-3 (hardbound) – ISBN 0-335-20320-5 (pbk.)
    1. Public welfare – Great Britain.   2. Public welfare – United States.   3. Great
Britain – Social policy – 1979.   4. United States – Social policy – 1993.   I. Title.
II. Series.

HV248.D33 2002
361.941–dc21   2001054508

Typeset by Type Study, Scarborough, North Yorkshire
Printed in Great Britain by St Edmundsbury Press, Bury St Edmunds, Suffolk

For Pat

Contents

Series editor's foreword

Welcome to the fourth volume in the Introducing Social Policy series. The series itself is designed to provide a range of well-informed texts on a wide variety of topics that fall within the ambit of social policy studies.

Although primarily designed with undergraduate social policy students in mind, it is hoped that the series – and individual titles within it – will have a wider appeal to students in other social science disciplines and to those engaged on professional and post-qualifying courses in health care and social welfare.

The aim throughout the planning of the series has been to produce a series of texts that both reflect and contribute to contemporary thinking and scholarship, and which present their discussion in a readable and easily accessible format.

Alan Deacon's contribution to the series provides a compelling and stimu-lating perspective on the current debates about welfare reform in Britain and the United States. In the process he provides a series of well-documented but accessible discussions of some of the principal thinkers of the present and the recent past. These include Richard Titmuss, the first Professor of Social Administration in a British university, who is best remembered for his view of welfare as an expression of altruism, and the American conservative Charles Murray, best known for his controversial studies of the underclass.

But the value of Deacon's study lies not only in his powers of exposition. It is the way he uses the theorists he has selected to highlight different per-spectives on what the role and purpose of welfare should be. Thus we are presented with welfare as an expression of altruism, a mechanism for moral regeneration and, perhaps most significantly for practical policies in Britain and the United States, welfare as a transition to work. Inequality, depen-dency and human agency are all integral to Deacon's study, which ends with a discussion of the mixed range of ideas that have shaped – and are shaping – recent and current policies on both sides of the Atlantic.

Alan Deacon's book represents an innovative contribution both to theoretical approaches and comparative studies in the discipline of social policy. Central to its message is the relationship between ideas and action, and between public policy and moral choice. It is a book which expounds the thinkers, presents the evidence and discusses the impact on policy programmes; but which, at the end, leaves its readers to make their own choice among the perspectives on welfare.

David Gladstone, University of Bristol

Acknowledgements

This book has taken an unconscionable time to write, and I am enormously grateful for the patience and enthusiasm of the series editor David Gladstone. I am also grateful for the advice and help of many friends and colleagues, including Peter Dwyer, David Green, Emma Heron, John Macnicol, Simon Robinson, Adrian Sinfield, Carol Smart, Steve Teles, Robert Walker, John Welshman, Robert Whelan and Michael Wiseman. I am particularly indebted to three colleagues in Leeds. Marie Leake read the whole book in draft and made many suggestions as to how it could be made more helpful to students. Kirk Mann has provided innumerable ideas, references and constructive criticisms over many years of friendship, and Fiona Williams has been both a supportive colleague and a constant source of stimulating and innovative ideas about welfare.

None of those whose work is discussed in this book were asked to comment upon it in draft. Nevertheless, I wish to thank Frank Field MP both for his personal kindness and for the interest that he has shown in my work over many years. I am also grateful to Lawrence Mead, who has been extraordinarily generous with his time and his research materials.

I am pleased to have an opportunity to acknowledge three sources of financial support. The first is the award of a Leverhulme Research Fellowship in 1998/9, which enabled me to undertake much of the research for Chapters 3 and 5. The second is a grant from the Rockefeller Foundation, which enabled me to present a paper on welfare reform in Britain and the United States to the 22nd Research Conference of the Association for Public Policy Analysis and Management in Seattle in November 2000. The third is the support of the Economic and Social Research Council for the Research Group on Care, Values and the Future of Welfare at the University of Leeds.

My preoccupation with welfare debates has long been tolerated with wry amusement by my daughters, Sarah and Rachel Deacon. My greatest debt, however, is to my partner Pat Fairfoot. She read every draft and was an unfailing source of ideas, encouragement and support. The book is dedicated to her with love and thanks.

List of abbreviations

AFDC	Aid to Families with Dependent Children
BHPS	British Household Panel Survey
CBPP	Center on Budget and Policy Priorities
CDF	Children's Defense Fund
CPAG	Child Poverty Action Group
DfEE	Department for Education and Employment
DSS	Department of Social Security
EITC	Earned Income Tax Credit
ESRC	Economic and Social Research Council
JWPTD	Joint Working Party into Transmitted Deprivation
LFP	Labour Force Participation
LSE	London School of Economics
NBTS	National Blood Transfusion Service
NDYP	New Deal for Young People
NHS	National Health Service
NWRO	National Welfare Rights Organization
PRWORA	Personal Responsibility and Work Opportunity Reconciliation Act
PSID	Panel Study of Income Dynamics
RCP	Responsive Communitarian Platform
SBC	Supplementary Benefits Commission
TANF	Temporary Assistance for Needy Families
WFTC	Working Families Tax Credit

Introduction

This book provides an introduction to the current debates about welfare reform in Britain and the United States. It starts from the premise that these debates reflect conflicting views of what constitutes a good society and what role welfare can play in bringing such a society into being. The first part of the book outlines five perspectives on welfare. Each of these perspectives offers a different formulation of what should be the role and purpose of welfare. They are not mutually exclusive, but each draws upon and articulates a different understanding of human nature and of the relationship between welfare and human behaviour and motivation.

- *Welfare as an expression of altruism.* This perspective assumes that the creation of a more equal and cohesive society will foster a sense of mutual obligation and help to realize the moral potentialities of its citizens. The task of welfare is to redistribute resources and opportunities, and thereby provide a framework for the encouragement and expression of altruism.
- *Welfare as a channel for the pursuit of self-interest.* This perspective assumes that the overwhelming majority of people who claim welfare will act rationally to better the conditions of themselves and their dependants. The task of welfare is to provide a framework of incentives that channels this desire for self-improvement in ways conducive to the common good.
- *Welfare as the exercise of authority.* This perspective starts from the premise that a significant proportion of claimants lack the capacities to pursue their own self-interest. In consequence they do not respond to changes in the framework of incentives in the way that the previous perspective assumes. The task of welfare is to compel such people to act in ways that are conducive to their long-term betterment, and hence to the common good.
- *Welfare as a transition to work.* This perspective has developed in

response to the previous two. It starts from the premise that cash benefits alone can never alleviate the problem of poverty. The more generous such benefits become, the more they undermine work incentives and threaten the stability of the family. The task of welfare should be to serve as a transition to paid employment.

- *Welfare as a mechanism for moral regeneration.* This perspective starts from the assumption that people are also motivated by a sense of commitment, and by an acceptance that they have obligations to the communities in which they live. The task of welfare is to foster and enhance this sense of duty, and it should look to do so through persuasion and moral argument.

The perspectives are explored through the writings of various academic and political commentators on welfare. Self-evidently, these commentators have been selected because they have provided a particularly persuasive or influential exposition of the different perspectives. There are, however, important differences between the individual writers, and these are reflected in the structure and format of the chapters that follow. It will be seen, for example, that some have spent their professional lives developing and promoting the perspective in question. In the case of other commentators, however, the writings discussed here are only part of a larger and more wide-ranging body of work. A further difference – and difficulty – is that although some of the commentators have remained consistent in their approach to welfare, others have shifted their ground over time or, in a few cases, have long held positions not entirely consistent with one another.

The differences between the individual commentators, however, are much less significant than what they have in common. They are all moralists. They all present arguments about what should be rather than analyses of what is. The broader social science literature has long distinguished between such normative or ideological approaches on the one hand, and analytical or theoretical approaches on the other. This distinction is not watertight, nor is it uncontested. As Pete Alcock (1996: 119–21) notes, however, it remains important for understanding the nature of debates about poverty and welfare. It will become clear, for example, that the writers discussed here formulate concepts and marshal evidence to give expression and weight to an argument, rather than to contribute to the development of theory. The outcome is what the American commentator Alice Rivlin (1973: 63) aptly termed 'forensic social science'. Everyone fights his or her own corner and assumes that everyone else is doing the same.

The implication of this is that the welfare debate is a highly polarized one. This was indeed the case in both Britain and the United States for much of the post-war period. During these years the debate was conducted from entrenched positions, and took the form of a mutual bombardment. There was little in the way of a genuine exchange of ideas, or even of hand-to-hand combat. In more recent times, however, the debate has become more complex and more reflective. The participants now adopt a greater diversity of positions, and some at least appear to be more willing to engage with opposing arguments and less inclined to dismiss them out of hand. One of the purposes of this book is to discuss why the welfare debate has changed in this way, and to consider the implications of this change for policy making. For now, however, there are a number of points that need to be made by way of introduction.

The first is that although the five perspectives that are outlined in Part 1 are quite distinct, they are not equally distant from one another. More specifically, there is a central difference between the perspective that is discussed first and the other four. The first perspective assumes that the central problem confronting welfare policy is inequality, whereas the other four assume the central problem to be one of dependency. It follows that the first perspective sees the primary task of welfare as to redistribute resources and opportunities. In contrast, the other four perspectives see the primary task of welfare as to lead people to act in ways that are more conducive to the common good and to their personal well-being. These four perspectives differ over how this can be achieved most effectively, and over the extent to which this will require some prior redistribution of resources. Nevertheless, they share a common concern with the behaviour and character of those who receive welfare – a concern which the first perspective regards as at best irrelevant and at worst pernicious. A corollary of this is that the first perspective is far more concerned with the identification and measurement of social need than are the other four.

The second point is that academic writing on welfare was long dominated by the first perspective. The extent of this domination is a matter of dispute, as is the degree to which it was reflected in the policies that were adopted by governments. What will become clear, however, is that the other four perspectives were consciously developed as critiques of the first perspective. Moreover, the collective impact of these critiques has been to fragment the welfare debate and to place the question of how welfare influences behaviour higher on the academic and political agenda.

The third point is that the fragmentation and greater fluidity of the welfare debate has been reflected in the welfare reforms introduced in both Britain and the United States. It will be shown in Part 2 that these reforms have drawn upon all the perspectives discussed in the book. Furthermore, it will be argued that the so-called 'third way' on welfare should be understood as an attempt to integrate and reconcile elements from the different perspectives.

Before proceeding further, however, it is important to be clear about the scope of the book, and to offer a preliminary justification for the approach that it takes. It can not be overemphasized that the central objective of the book is not to provide a comprehensive account of the development and implementation of welfare policies, but to convey the compelling and absorbing nature of the moral debates that underpin the formulation of those policies. This in turn, however, raises two questions that must be answered at the outset. First, what is meant by 'welfare'? Second, what is the justification for such an emphasis upon ideas and perspectives? Why do these moral debates merit a book?

What is welfare?

There are few words in the social sciences that are used as inconsistently as 'welfare'. The first complication is that it has different meanings when used on its own and when used as part of the term 'the welfare state'.

In British usage the phrase 'a welfare state' customarily refers to a society in which the government accepts responsibility for ensuring that all its citizens receive a minimum income, and have access to the highest possible provision in the fields of health care, housing, education and personal social services. This responsibility is discharged most directly through a range of 'social services'. These social services developed during the first half of the twentieth century, but they were transformed in scope and quality during and immediately after the Second World War. In the words of the historian Rodney Lowe, the British welfare state was 'the unique creation of the 1940s' (Lowe 1999: 13). As such it embodied the collectivist and egalitarian ethos that had been engendered by wartime conditions, and was characterized by the 'two ideals of universalism and comprehensiveness'. 'For the first time in history *all* citizens were to be insured "from the cradle to the grave" against *every* eventuality which might lead to the inadvertent loss of their income' (p. 13).

At least some of these 'eventualities', however, can also be covered in other ways. Benefits provided by employers, for example, provide income during periods of sickness, or in retirement. Similarly, tax reliefs and allowances can help to meet the costs of children, or subsidize the purchase of houses or of private medical insurance. Welfare policy, then, is usually seen as encompassing the government's stance towards such occupational and fiscal welfare, as well as the benefits and services that it provides itself.

This, of course, raises the fundamental question: who are these 'citizens'? Is this protection really afforded to everyone, or is it limited by gender, race or physical and intellectual capacities? These questions were often ignored in the literature on social policy (Williams 1989). So too was the question of what constitutes a minimum income, or what represents the highest possible standard in health care or education. As John Viet Wilson (2000: 1) has pointed out, theorists such as Esping-Anderson and Offe have failed to develop any criteria with which to distinguish welfare states from non-welfare states, and the term has been 'emptied of any explanatory meaning'.

The second complication is that in Britain the word 'welfare' has effectively lost one meaning and acquired another. For much of the post-war period it was synonymous with social work, or, more accurately, the personal social services provided by local authorities. In 1976, for example, Phoebe Hall published a study of the reorganization of these services under the title *Reforming the Welfare*. In the late 1960s, however, the word began to be used to refer to the means-tested social security benefits paid to the poorest households. Among the first to talk about welfare in this way were Tony Lynes, David Bull and others associated with the Child Poverty Action Group (CPAG), which had been founded in 1965 to campaign on behalf of poor families. Their objective was to establish a legal entitlement to such benefits and thereby give them a status comparable to that of contributory insurance benefits. They were inspired by the apparent success of the 'welfare rights' campaign conducted in the United States by the National Welfare Rights Organization (NWRO), and in seeking to emulate the success of the American activists they also adopted their terminology (Bull 2000: x).

In the United States welfare has always meant one thing: means-tested assistance paid primarily to lone mothers and their children. This assistance is paid in the form of food stamps and cash benefits, and for many years the most important programme of cash assistance was Aid to Families with Dependent Children (AFDC). In 1996, however, AFDC was abolished and replaced with a radically different programme called Temporary Assistance for Needy Families (TANF). It will be seen in Chapter 6 that the passage and implementation of the 1996 Act aroused intense controversy. Indeed welfare reform was a central issue in American politics for much of the decade, even though it accounts for only 8 per cent of total income transfers in the USA. Moreover, it will be argued later that this debate has had a profound impact upon thinking about welfare in Britain, and especially upon the approach to welfare reform adopted by the New Labour government. This influence is reflected in the language used, and one consequence of what Robert Walker has termed the 'Americanization of the British welfare debate' has been the adoption of American terminology (Walker 1998a: 32). Now when ministers talk of welfare dependency, or of welfare to work programmes, they are usually referring to cash benefits paid to people of working age. On other occasions and in other contexts, however, those same ministers have used 'welfare' interchangeably with welfare state, or even social services.

It is impossible to eliminate such inconsistencies from this book. In general, the American writers base their prescriptions upon analyses of welfare in the narrow sense, whereas Richard Titmuss and the other earlier commentators present a vision of the welfare state as a broader entity. In every case, however, the purpose is to provide as clear an outline as possible of the perspective, not to trim and twist them to conform to a rigid pro-forma. What is most important about the Americanization of the debate is not the change of language, but the new moralism which that language reflects.

The nature of welfare debates

The key to understanding the nature of the welfare debate in the United States is to appreciate the very sharp distinction that exists between welfare on the one hand and social security and Medicare on the other. Social security comprises a set of contributory programmes that provide old age, survivors, disability and unemployment insurance, while Medicare provides health insurance for the elderly. On the relatively rare occasions when American commentators refer to the 'US welfare state' they usually mean a combination of social security and Medicare.

The crucial point here, however, is that the key issues in debates about social security and Medicare are the coverage of the programmes, the level of the benefits they provide and how and by whom they are to be funded. Policy making in this area is essentially an exercise in striking a balance between conflicting interests and pressures, and among the pressures that have to be accommodated are those exerted by benefit recipients themselves, most notably by the 'grey lobby' in the case of benefits for the elderly.

The position in respect of welfare is wholly different. As Steve Teles (1996: 12) has argued, the debate around AFDC and TANF is 'an almost pure case of cultural and intellectual politics'. This is because the NWRO was a short-lived exception to the 'general rule' that 'the poor play no direct role in the politics of welfare in America'.

> Because of the absence of any interest group or other organized political role for the poor in the politics of welfare, the vacuum is filled by those who either claim to speak for the poor or who posses some form of expertise or higher understanding that permits them to know what a properly functioning welfare system would look like.
>
> (Teles 1996: 16)

It follows that 'the interests at issue in welfare policy making are only tangentially those of recipients themselves: the more important interests are those of the non-poor.' Moreover, Teles goes on to argue that welfare raises fundamental questions about the rights and obligations of citizenship, and about the scope and purpose of public policy. 'It concerns not merely who gets what, when, where, and how, but why a particular community exists and for what ends it is organized' (p. 17). The inevitable consequence is that welfare politics is 'exceptionally dominated by issues of morality' (p. 16). Does welfare undermine personal responsibility and lead people to look more readily to others for support? Does the payment of welfare to lone mothers encourage the break-up of two-parent families?

These are not, of course, the only questions that can be asked about welfare. Far more attention could be paid to whether or not it lifts people out of poverty, or improves their physical and mental health. Conversely, neither the alleged break-down of the family nor the erosion of the work ethic are confined to those on welfare. Nevertheless, the well documented hostility of the American public to welfare claimants means that it is welfare that provides the prime focus for the discussion of such issues and for the public expression of such anxieties.

The British public is similarly hostile to some groups of benefit claimants. In general, however, more comprehensive coverage of the means-tested social assistance scheme means that there is not the same distinction between 'welfare' and 'social security' as there is in the USA. In consequence, the twin issues of what benefits cost and how they impact upon the family and the labour market are interwoven much more closely in the British debates. That said, it will be seen in Chapter 7 that the debate in Britain has become far more concerned with moral issues in recent years. Moreover, it is a central argument of this book that this shift is due in large part to the impact of the perspectives discussed here. This, however, is a very big claim, and is one that other scholars would challenge.

The importance of welfare debates

This book is open to the criticism that it overstates the role and significance of ideas in the development of welfare policy. Alvin Schoor (1984: 403), for example, has written scathingly of those whose 'preoccupation with moral strictures floats above the surface of class and partisan interest, as if the cocktail party and gossip on deck determined the course of the ship'. At the root of developments, he argues, is a 'distributive struggle, framed and re-framed by economic forces and social structure, which may wax and wane but does not end' (p. 405).

An immediate response to such a challenge is that the writers discussed in the following chapters do not claim that they can explain why welfare takes the forms that it does. Instead their objective is to set out a convincing prescription for policy in the future. This, however, is open to the further objection that such writers have little influence upon policy. On this view, the question is not whether the gossip on the deck determines the course of the ship but whether the captain and crew take any notice of it at all. Part 2 of the book attempts to meet this objection, at least in part. It was noted above that it documents the impact of the welfare debate upon the reforms recently introduced in both Britain and the United States. In particular, it shows how those reforms were formulated in response to specific arguments about welfare dependency, and how they explicitly sought to reach an accommodation with those arguments.

This, however, does not provide a full justification for the approach taken in this book. It is still possible to acknowledge that the direction of welfare reform reflects the *Zeitgeist*, or spirit of the times, but to argue that the *Zeitgeist* is itself the product of forces far broader than the impact of a few key thinkers. This, for example, is the basis of the strong criticisms that David Donnison (2000) has made of an earlier article by the present author and a colleague (Deacon and Mann 1999). Donnison's charge is that the article in question greatly exaggerates the influence of Richard Titmuss. He does not dispute that many academics working in the fields of social and urban policy in the 1960s and 1970s 'had a cast of mind which equipped them to pose particular questions and to seek particular answers'. Donnison goes on to argue, however, that this cast of mind cannot be 'attributed to the influence of one man – even a man as outstanding as Titmuss'. A far more plausible explanation is that it was 'their shared history of the depression, the poor laws, the war, and other formative experiences which led them to espouse the same hopes'. The same was true of the 'policy culture' of the 'New Right' that took over in the following generation. This was shaped not by 'any charismatic individual but by common features of a different kind of economy and the different social structures it sustained' (Donnison 2000: 40–1).

The specific case of Titmuss is discussed in the next chapter. In general, however, there are two further points that should be made in response to this criticism. The first is that the book does not assume that 'big ideas' simply emerge in a vacuum. On the contrary, it attempts to understand the development of each perspective within the broader context that Donnison outlines. As David Marquand (1996: 6) has put it, 'academic scribblers respond to the pressures of the society around them, and their scribbles resonate only when they speak to social forces.' The second point is that governments do not arrive in office with a clearly formulated programme that they then proceed to implement in full and in detail. Instead policies are fashioned and refashioned through the interplay between ideas and events, between political commitments and the experience of administration, and between values and the exigencies of office and electoral politics. As David Marquand has again written,

> if thought influences action, action also influences thought . . . Belief and behaviour, ideas and policies, visions of the future and legacies of the past, form a seamless web; attempts to unpick it, to give primacy to thought over action, or to action over thought, confuse more than they illuminate
>
> (Marquand 1996: 6)

This book does not try to 'unpick' this web, and it makes no attempt to assess the significance of ideas relative to that of other factors. It argues that the thinking of academic and political commentators is shaped by social forces, but that it is not determined by those forces. It asserts that ideas matter, even though they are not the only things that matter.

There is, however, a further and still more important justification for the focus of this book upon perspectives on welfare, and the debates between those perspectives. This is not that particular arguments about equality or dependency have influenced the direction of welfare reform. Rather, it is that those arguments raise issues that are of enduring interest to students of welfare.

As Fiona Williams (2000: 1) has written, one of the reasons why social policy is such an exciting subject is that it 'holds the big questions and the small details of our lives together in one frame'. 'How a society organises and manages the welfare of its citizens tells us about its social and economic priorities, its hierarchies, its inequalities, its cultural practices, and its response to change.' 'Above all', she argues, welfare is about the 'moral choices we face'. These moral choices arise in public policy, as they do in social practices and in personal relationships. What 'are our responsibilities one for another? Who represents the "our" and who "the other"?' (p. 1). In this way, she adds, the study of welfare confronts the 'central ethical question each society must answer': 'Am I my brother's – or my sister's – keeper?'

This question has often been posed, but in reality it begs a host of other questions. Who are these 'brothers and sisters'? Is this 'family' universal, or is it delineated by citizenship of nation states, or, more narrowly, by membership of communities of place or faith, or even by kinship? In what manner are these brothers and sisters to be kept? Do they owe anything in return? Is there a danger that by 'keeping' our brothers and sisters, we make them more dependent upon 'us'? Is it sometimes a mark of respect to insist that they do more to help themselves? Or are such questions rendered pointless by the gross inequalities that remain in the resources and opportunities open to different 'brothers and sisters'?

What is most striking and most interesting about the writers who are the subject of this book is the way in which they make explicit this link between public policy and moral choice. Each begins by asking questions such as these, and each bases his or her policy prescriptions upon moral arguments about what are and what are not the proper objectives of welfare policy. Nowhere is this link made more clearly or expressed more powerfully than in the work of Richard Titmuss.

Further reading

Excellent accounts of the development of the British welfare state since 1945 are provided by Glennerster (2000b), Lowe (1999) and Timmins (1996). The structure of welfare in the USA prior to the reforms of the 1990s is outlined in the early chapters of Bryner (1998) and Weaver (2000). The differences and similarities between the two welfare regimes are discussed by Dolwitz (1997), King (1995) and Deacon (2000, 2001). Different interpretations of the role of ideas in the policy-making process are offered by Donnison (2000), Seldon (1996) and Teles (1996). *The Ideas that Shaped Post-war Britain* is the title of a particularly interesting set of essays edited by Marquand and Seldon (1996).

PART 1

The perspectives

chapter

one

Welfare and equality

This chapter outlines three perspectives on welfare. These three perspectives are discussed in the same chapter because they have much in common. They all assume that a central goal of welfare is to reduce inequalities, and they all reject any attempt to explain the growth or persistence of poverty in terms of the behaviour and attitudes of poor people themselves. Together, these perspectives dominated thinking about welfare for much of the post-war period, both in Britain and in America. It will be seen, however, that these perspectives are based upon subtly different assumptions about human nature and motivation.

The perspective that is explored in the first part of this chapter starts from the premise that people are often motivated by a regard for the concerns and needs of others. It argues that the primary purpose of welfare is to foster and encourage these feelings of altruism and to give expression to them. In order to fulfil this purpose, however, welfare must first contribute to a broader redistribution of resources and opportunities. This is because a reduction in social inequalities is a precondition for the creation of a common culture and for the establishment of social relationships based upon altruism. Moreover, this redistribution can and must be achieved through social services which are themselves non-discriminatory and which foster a sense of community. At the heart of this perspective, then, is the belief that resources must be channelled to the poor within an infrastructure of benefits and services that are open to and used by all. As far as possible, entitlement to welfare should be universal and unconditional. It should not depend upon the incomes of claimants, and claimants should not be required to meet conditions regarding their behaviour or their character.

The most powerful and most influential exposition of this first perspective is to be found in the work of Richard Titmuss. It is widely acknowledged, however, that Titmuss's influence upon the British welfare debate continued long after his death in 1973, and the second part of the chapter goes on to discuss briefly the development of the so-called Titmuss paradigm or Titmuss school. It is argued here, however, that this is more properly understood as a 'quasi-Titmuss' paradigm or school.[1] This is because it became increasingly preoccupied with the growth of material inequalities and paid correspondingly less attention to altruism and the quality of social relationships. Because the quasi-Titmuss paradigm paid less attention to altruism it also paid less attention than Titmuss had done to the question of how far people's behaviours and activities represented some form of meaningful choice, what came to be known later as the issue of human agency.

Titmuss himself had fiercely rejected any attempt to explain poverty in terms of the failings or weaknesses of the poor themselves. In the quasi-Titmuss paradigm, however, this rejection of individualist or **behavioural** accounts of poverty hardened and broadened into a more determinist approach that, in effect, precluded any discussion of such factors. The defining characteristic of the quasi-Titmuss paradigm, then, is that it is uninterested in questions of agency and is hostile to the idea that one of the purposes of welfare is to shape the behaviours and aspirations of those who receive it.

A similar hostility to discussions of behaviour is to be found in much American writing on welfare in the 1970s. In the USA, however, the rejection of behavioural explanations of poverty was given a special intensity by the impact of the civil rights movement. The fact that poverty was concentrated upon black and Hispanic Americans reinforced the hostility of many commentators to accounts that appeared to 'blame the victim'. It will be seen in the third part of this chapter that this American egalitarianism expresses in an even sharper form the denial of agency that characterizes the quasi-Titmuss paradigm.

In both countries, however, the reluctance – even refusal – of the dominant perspectives to debate or even to discuss issues of behaviour and choice created a vacuum that was later filled by conservative ideas about welfare dependency and about an underclass.

Richard Titmuss: welfare and altruism

It will be seen that many of the writers discussed in this book have had highly unorthodox careers, and that it is impossible to locate their work within conventional academic boundaries. Few, however, have had as remarkable a life as Richard Titmuss.

He was born in 1907, the son of a farmer, and left school at 14 without the equivalent of a single GCSE. Following a course on bookkeeping at his local college and a spell as an office boy, he became a clerk in an insurance office. Titmuss held a full-time job in commercial insurance for the next 16 years. From the early 1930s, however, he became increasingly interested in social and political issues. These interests were further stimulated and given new direction by his wife Kay, who was prominent in the organization of clubs for the unemployed when they met in 1934. By 1939 Titmuss was the author or co-author of two books and numerous essays and articles on public health, food policy and the threat to national well-being posed by the apparent decline in the population. The interest aroused by these writings led to an invitation at the end of 1941 to begin work on the official history of the wartime social services. Titmuss was to publish two further books during the war but it was the publication of his official history in 1950 that was to establish his professional reputation. *Problems of Social Policy* was hailed as a masterpiece and led directly to a further invitation from the University of London to become Britain's first Professor of Social Administration at the London School of Economics.

Titmuss was to remain at the LSE for the rest of his life, and was to have a profound influence upon academic thinking about welfare for over twenty years. As Robert Pinker (1977: vii) has commented, 'few scholars have so dominated the development of an academic subject over so long a period of time as did Richard Titmuss.' He was also to have a significant influence upon public policy, not only in Britain but also in the USA and some African countries. This influence was due in large part to the quality of Titmuss's own writings. In Margaret Gowing's words, he was 'one of the few truly original social scientists of his generation' who 'asked questions of great conceptual importance which had not occurred to anyone else but which thereafter seemed obvious' (Gowing 1975: 401, 404).

The significance of Titmuss's ideas, however, also stems from his influence upon the research of others. This influence was itself a reflection of Titmuss's personal charisma; his ability to infuse others with his own intense belief in the value of his subject and his own moral commitment and certainties. In a generally unsympathetic account of Titmuss, John Vaizey (1983: 61) referred to a 'resonance, the ability to hint at the inexpressible, at a complex pattern of ideas and values to which kindred spirits would feel attracted.' It was this, Vaizey suggested, that explained the intense loyalty that Titmuss inspired in others.

Titmuss shaped the development of social policy as an academic subject in two ways. First, he broadened its scope. Before the Second World War, courses in social administration had focused almost entirely upon the origins and administration of statutory social services, and were taken almost solely by people who intended to work in those services. Titmuss did more than anyone else to uncouple this link and to establish social policy as a subject in its own right. In particular, he argued that it was wrong to look at state benefits in isolation from occupational benefits or tax reliefs granted in respect of similar needs. His famous essay on the social division of welfare remains one of the most widely read articles in social policy and has formed the basis of many subsequent analyses of the distribution and impact of welfare (Sinfield 1978; Mann 1992).

Second, and more importantly for this book, Titmuss redefined the purpose and focus of the subject. What interested and animated him above all else were the moral choices that underlay policy decisions. All that research and enquiry could do was to identify options: the real issue was the values that shaped the objectives of policy.

Titmuss, Tawney and equality

It is widely recognized that Titmuss's thinking was profoundly influenced by that of Richard Tawney.

Richard Tawney was a distinguished economic historian but he is now best remembered as the author of several books and essays that set out the case for equality from the standpoint of Christian Socialism. Tawney started from the premise that everyone was entitled to equality of respect by virtue of their common relationship to their Creator. Two things followed from this. The first was the principle that everyone is entitled to the resources and opportunities they need to develop to the limit of their potential. The second was the idea of fellowship, and it is the latter which is generally regarded as the pivotal concept in Tawney's thought.

Tawney's understanding of fellowship is complex, and rooted in Christian notions of *agape* or love. In essence, however, it represents the kinds of social relationships that follow from an acceptance that all are of equal value; that all merit the same respect and consideration. For Tawney such relationships are

> incompatible with the existence of sharp contrasts between the economic standards and educational opportunities of different classes, for such contrasts have as their result, not a common culture, but servility or resentment, on the one hand, and patronage or arrogance, on the other.
>
> (Quoted in Reisman 1982: 25)

The most powerful case for equality, then, was that it was essential for the development of a sense of common purpose, without which a community 'is not a community at all' (Reisman 1982: 25).

Titmuss did not share Tawney's Christian faith, but he did share fully Tawney's belief that the first step 'towards an improvement in social life is to judge our social conduct by strict moral standards'. There are, Tawney had insisted, 'certain sorts of behaviour which we know to be right, and certain others which we know to be wrong' (Reisman 1982: 80). Like Tawney's, Titmuss's primary concern was to create the social and economic conditions in which 'right behaviours' would be fostered and sustained and in which fellowship could flourish. As David Reisman (1982: 75) has concluded, 'It is through the Tawney–Titmuss relationship that the British tradition of common culture became translated into a demand for social welfare firmly rooted in shared social values.'

Before going further it must be acknowledged that neither Titmuss nor Tawney paid any attention to social divisions based upon gender. As Ann Oakley (1997: 4) has written, Titmuss 'signally failed to notice the deep fissure in the vision of an equal society created by men's and women's different social experiences.' His was an 'analysis of a welfare system divided on the axis of occupational class: the discovery of differentiation by gender had to await its own historical moment' (Oakley 1991: 188).

Titmuss and unconditional welfare

Titmuss's central argument was that welfare, broadly understood, had a unique potential to achieve two objectives at the same time. First, it could redistribute resources and thereby lessen inequalities; second, it could bring about this redistribution through processes and institutions which themselves contributed to social integration and encouraged fellowship. He wrote in his last book, *The Gift Relationship*, that the defining quality of welfare was its focus upon 'integrative systems: on processes, transactions and institutions which promote an individual's sense of identity, participation and community' (Titmuss 1970: 224).

In order to realize its potential for integration, however, welfare had to fulfil two criteria. It had to be universal and it had to be non-judgemental. Benefits and services which were available only to the poor, or which attempt to distinguish between the deserving and the undeserving, would serve only to divide and to alienate. Titmuss believed that all of this had been demonstrated during the Second World War, and *Problems of Social Policy* was part social history and part a 'declaration of faith in communal action through the government' (Gowing 1975: 410).

Titmuss argued that the circumstances of war led to a profound shift in British public opinion. The experience of common sacrifice and effort created a fierce resentment of privilege and a refusal to return to the social divisions and inequalities of the 1930s. He believed that two episodes had been especially important. The first was the evacuation of school children from the cities to the middle-class suburbs and the countryside. This had led initially to a flood of complaints about verminous children and feckless parents, but in the longer term it had destroyed the mutual ignorance of the social classes. The second episode that Titmuss highlighted was the fall of France and the retreat from Dunkirk. Everyone now faced the prospect of invasion and occupation, and 'if dangers were to be shared, then resources should also be shared' (Titmuss 1950: 508).

Titmuss went on to show how public policies were transformed in response to the 'war-warmed impulse of people for a more generous society'

(1950: 508). The most significant change was that 'individual distress' was no longer regarded 'as a mark of social incapacity' (p. 506). There was, for example, no disgrace in being bombed out by the enemy, and the provision for those rendered destitute by air raids was in sharp contrast to the treatment of the unemployed or homeless before the war. It was, Titmuss concluded, the 'less constraining, less discriminating scope and quality of the war-time social services' that was the key to their effectiveness (p. 506).

Titmuss's interpretation of the war years has been challenged by later historians (Welshman 1999). What matters here, however, is the way in which his perception of these events shaped his thinking on welfare. His commitment to universalism, for example, led him to dismiss attempts to target resources on the poor through means tests. For Titmuss the most important defect of means testing was that it divided society into two groups: those who were eligible for benefits and services and those who saw themselves as paying for them. Among other things this led him to be critical of the American War on Poverty programmes. These, he said, were an attempt to 'reach the poor directly and concentrate resources on them without the support of an infrastructure of social welfare utilized and approved by the non-poor as well as the poor' (Titmuss 1968: 113). They had been introduced with the best of intentions, but their advocates had failed to appreciate the extent to which 'these programmes would require the poor to define themselves: to stand up and declare themselves poor people' (p. 113).

Of still greater significance for this book, however, was Titmuss's insistence that welfare be non-judgemental. In his inaugural lecture in 1951 Titmuss had quoted with approval Tawney's 'warning' that the 'problem of poverty is not a problem of individual character and its waywardness, but a problem of economic and industrial organisation' (Titmuss 1958b: 18). He was later to develop the argument that welfare should be understood as a form of compensation paid to those who bore the social costs of the technological and industrial change wrought by economic growth. In part, he wrote, it may represent 'a compensation for disservices caused by society'. If the social costs of 'disservices', such as the obsolescence of skills, industrial injuries, poor housing and environmental pollution, were not to lie where they fell 'then we have to find ways and means of compensating people without stigma' (Titmuss 1968: 117).

The issue of stigma was one to which Titmuss returned again and again. By stigma he meant the 'spoiled identity' or 'felt and experienced discrimination and disapproval' which resulted from being castigated as a public burden. The fundamental challenge, then, was to redistribute social rights without stigma, and this could not be done through welfare systems that started from the premise that the poor were incompetent or feckless.

Titmuss, however, did not rule out the possibility that there was a small minority of people whose poverty could be attributed to their own behaviour, at least in part. In the 1930s he had been sympathetic to the idea that there was a social problem group (Titmuss 1938: 288), and in *Problems of Social Policy* he took up the question of how far the experience of evacuation had confirmed the existence of such families. His conclusion was that no more than 5 per cent were 'problem children from problem homes'. Many of the others may have 'preferred chips to green vegetables' and had 'dirty heads', but 'such things do not mean that they belonged to the social problem group' (Titmuss 1950: 135). What is particularly striking in the context of this chapter, however, is Titmuss's dismissal as 'silly' those Labour MPs who complained that 'any mention of lice' was a slur on the working class. 'The louse is not a political creature: it cannot distinguish between the salt of the earth and the scum of the earth' (p. 136).

Comments such as these have led the historian John Welshman to locate *Problems of Social Policy* within a broader wartime literature that was 'ambivalent' in its approach to poverty. Welshman argues that this literature incorporated both 'behavioural and environmental components', and that it is 'an unhelpful way of viewing social policy in the 1940s' to suggest that there was simple divide between 'reactionary' and 'radical' explanations of poverty (Welshman 1999: 807).

In his later work Titmuss acknowledged that welfare systems had to avoid 'building in disincentives to full time work and disincentives to the stability of marriage and family responsibilities' (Titmuss 1987: 230). In a lecture in 1967, however, he argued that the need for effective policies had to be set against the 'rights of the consumer to certain services irrespective of their morals and patterns of behaviour' (Titmuss 1968: 69).

In some cases he favoured the more 'effective' option. The most striking example was the advice he gave to the colonial government in Mauritius (Reisman 1977: 17, 96). Confronted with a pressing need to restrain a burgeoning birth rate in a predominately Catholic country, Titmuss proposed a benefits system that penalized early marriage and large families. Most strikingly of all, he recommended that family allowances be withheld from fourth and subsequent children, a provision that was akin to the family cap that was to prove so controversial in the USA more than thirty years later (and which is discussed in Chapter 6). Although 'painfully stern', these measures were indeed effective. In 1971 the rate of population growth was little more than one-third of what it had been in 1956 (Gowing 1975: 421).

In general, however, Titmuss was more concerned to protect the rights and freedoms of individuals. In his last ever course of lectures he told his students that Swedish experience had shown that it was possible for public agencies to recover from absent fathers a substantial proportion of the monies paid to the mothers of their children. The price of this 'success', however, could be a 'failure to preserve privacy and the freedom to disappear for a majority of citizens' (Titmuss 1974: 54).

The most important point to make here, however, is that these were not issues to which Titmuss devoted much attention, and when he did they were treated as largely abstract dilemmas with little relevance to policy. In a paper first published in 1970, for example, he specifically rejected the notion that there could be 'some kind of final solution' to the problems of social security, and quoted with approval Isaiah Berlin on the misplaced hopes – and worse – which stemmed from the 'ancient faith' that 'all the positive values in which men have believed must in the end be compatible' (Titmuss 1987: 220).

Titmuss's disinclination to dwell on these questions was reinforced by two other aspects of his thought. One of these was his optimism about the implications of future economic performance. In 1965 he argued that in 'an age of abundance' the 'production of consumption goods will become a subsidiary question for the West. The primary question will be just distribution.' By 'just distribution' Titmuss meant replacing the 'principle of productivity and performance in a market economy' by the principle of distribution according to need (Titmuss 1987: 124). It was much more important to ask what 'are we to do with our wealth?' than it was to ask how we can prevent the abuse of public assistance, or force men to look for work, or compel them to save for old age (p. 124). The current role of social workers, teachers or social administrators was to police virtues of hard work and thrift that were 'rooted in the economics of scarcity' and had 'no relevance to the economics of abundance' (p. 125).

Still more remarkable, however, was Titmuss's optimism regarding human nature. It must be stressed that this optimism did not emerge in the 1960s but was a prominent feature of his early writings. *Parents Revolt*, for example, was published in 1942. Co-written with Kay Titmuss, this claimed that the decline in the birth rate represented a rejection of the 'virus of acquisitiveness' that was engendered by capitalism. There could be no solution to the problems posed by a declining population, they argued, as long as 'each individual follows his own interests, is taught to serve himself and not others, and is forced by the character of the environment in which he moves to act acquisitively and not co-operatively' (Titmuss 1942: 120). What were needed were new values that 'will release that deep, long-frustrated desire in man to serve humanity and not self' (p. 122).

By far the most influential expression of this argument, however, came in Titmuss's last book, *The Gift Relationship* (1970). In this book Titmuss contrasted the National Blood Transfusion Service (NBTS) in Britain with the operation of commercial markets for blood in other countries, particularly the United States. He claimed to have demonstrated that the blood supplied by voluntary donors was far superior in terms of its purity and the dependability of its supply than that obtained from commercial donors. These findings had an enormous impact. *The New York Times* selected *The Gift Relationship* as one of the best seven books of 1971, and it went to become a best-seller. Elliot Richardson, then Secretary of State for Health, Education and Welfare, consulted Titmuss personally over the reform of the blood banks in the USA. As a result of those reforms the share of the blood market taken by commercial blood banks fell from 30 to 5 per cent during the 1970s (Oakley and Ashton 1997: 6).

For Titmuss the all-important point was that those who donated to the NBTS in Britain were 'free not to give'. They could 'have behaved differently': 'Their decisions were not determined by structure or by function or controlled by ineluctable historical forces. They were not compelled, coerced, bribed or paid to give' (Titmuss 1970: 239). Their actions represented a 'practical and concrete demonstration' of fellowship, which Tawney had always understood as a 'matter of right relationships which are institutionally based'. In this case that institution was the NHS. The 'most unsordid Act of British social policy in the twentieth century', it was the NHS that 'allowed and encouraged sentiments of altruism, reciprocity and social duty to express themselves' (Titmuss 1970: 225). It did so, moreover, because the structure and function of the NHS itself was not socially divisive. Titmuss provided a moving illustration of what this meant in practice at the end of one of the last lectures he ever gave. Describing the treatment he had received for cancer, he spoke of a

young West Indian from Trinidad, aged twenty five, with cancer of the rectum. His appointment was the same as mine for radium treatment – ten o' clock every day. Sometimes he went into the Theatron Room first, sometimes I did. What determined waiting was quite simply the vagaries of London traffic, not race, not religion, not class, not colour.
(Titmuss 1974: 150–1)

In *The Gift Relationship*, however, Titmuss went on to argue that the NHS was but one example of how social policy could 'facilitate the expression of man's moral sense', and thereby 'help to actualize the social and moral potentialities of all citizens' (Titmuss 1970: 238). Titmuss also spoke of a 'social and biological need to help' that was curtailed by market relationships but 'safeguarded and extended' by 'non-discriminatory social institutions' (p. 243). This optimism, however, would not have been shared by Tawney himself. As Simon Robinson has pointed out, Tawney held a 'Christian view of man as sinful as well as capable of compassion'. This precluded 'any simple appeal to, or reliance upon, altruism' and led Tawney to 'stress responsibilities and duties rather than rights'. In contrast, writes Robinson, 'Titmuss's view of humanity' was 'far more optimistic'. In consequence, Robinson argues, Titmuss's moralism 'emphasizes the duties of the state to the individual and not the obligations of the individual' (Robinson 1987: 190).

Similarly, the theologian Ronald Preston has argued that Titmuss is among those who

have been misled by the utopian element in Tawney's thought (without noting his qualifications). They often make the mistake of stressing only the dignity of man; they underplay his sinfulness. This . . . has the effect of presenting people of conservative disposition with an entirely unnecessary weapon.

(Preston 1979: 109)

Preston's criticism is particularly apposite in respect of Titmuss's neglect of the labour market. It was here that Titmuss's optimism regarding human nature combined with his belief that economic success was no longer as dependent upon the maintenance of the work ethic or labour discipline. This led him to dismiss what he termed the 'handmaiden' model of welfare, which was derived from 'various economic and psychological theories concerned with incentive, effort and reward' (Titmuss 1974: 31). Nor was he sympathetic to the idea that the unemployed should be required to participate in work or training programmes as a condition of benefit. As Miller notes, Titmuss believed that such conditions turned welfare into an instrument of economic policy – a 'distortion' of what 'social policies are about' (Miller 1987: 12).

It is true that Titmuss's acceptance of public office – particularly as Deputy Chairman of the Supplementary Benefits Commission – meant that he had to make a greater accommodation than he may have wished to public concerns with benefit abuse or work incentives. In his academic work, however, such concerns were scarcely considered. The ambivalence of the immediate post-war years had largely gone. The irrelevance of behavioural analyses had been demonstrated and they did not merit further enquiry. In a lecture to the inaugural meeting of the then Social Administration Association in 1967 he set out the eight major fields of teaching and research in the subject. None referred specifically to the labour market (Titmuss 1968: 22–3). This was not something in which Titmuss had any interest, and under his influence academic social policy paid it little attention.

The quasi-Titmuss paradigm: welfare and redistribution

Writing shortly after Titmuss's death, T. H. Marshall noted that he had come to exert an influence 'which has not been surpassed by any British social scientist of his generation'. He went on to observe that Titmuss's direct personal influence was 'magnified and multiplied by transmission through' his colleagues and former students, 'many of whom before he died were occupying Chairs and teaching posts throughout the land' (Marshall 1973: 137). Titmuss's former colleagues continued to occupy these positions for many years after his death. As David Donnison, one of the most distinguished of them, has recalled, those working in academic social policy 'found that they had joined a club, linked intellectually (and often personally) by what amounted to a shared ideology' (Donnison 1979: 146). That ideology is generally characterized as the Titmuss paradigm or Titmuss school. Hilary Rose, for example, wrote in 1981 that at 'its height the Titmuss school reigned unchallenged over the construction of social policy' (Rose 1981: 484).

In some respects, however, it would be more accurate to call this the quasi-Titmuss paradigm or school. This is because the ideology shared by this club came to differ from that developed and expounded by Titmuss himself. Even those most closely associated with Titmuss during his lifetime found some of his ideas more persuasive than others. In general, they found his arguments for unconditional welfare more convincing than his belief in altruism. They may have agreed in principle that, in Rose's words, altruism was the 'highest moment of the social relations of redistribution' (p. 489). In practice, however, they were less concerned than Titmuss to foster feelings of altruism or a sense of community, and they paid less attention to the moral case for equality. Whereas Titmuss had seen greater equality primarily as a means of transforming social relationships, the quasi-Titmuss school viewed it as a matter of distributive justice, and regarded the need to redistribute income and wealth as largely self-evident. Above all, the quasi-Titmuss school extended Titmuss's repudiation of individualist explanations of social problems into a more developed account of how the resources and opportunities open to people depended not upon their attitudes or behaviour but upon their position in the social structure. This perspective is exemplified in Townsend's massively influential studies of poverty and deprivation (Townsend 1979; Deacon and Mann 1999: 416).

It was argued in the Introduction that changes in ideas and ideologies are never straightforward, and that they cannot be viewed in a vacuum. The shift in emphasis between the Titmuss paradigm and the quasi-Titmuss paradigm is no exception. There was no simple transition from one to the other, and there was always a substantial overlap between them. Broadly speaking, however, it is possible to identify four factors that shaped the quasi-Titmuss paradigm.

The first was the growing influence upon the welfare debate of Marxist political economy. This focused upon collective rather than individual action, and paid far more attention to the development of theory. Writers in this so-called critical social policy tradition criticized Titmuss's work for what Peter Taylor-Gooby (1981: 7) called its 'uncritical empiricism'. Titmuss's neglect of social class was said to render him unable to understand the structural causes of the social inequalities he described, and his preoccupation with ideas and values was said to leave him unable to formulate a coherent strategy for effecting change (Lee and Raban 1988).

A second, very different, influence was that of the Labour politician and theorist of social democracy Anthony Crosland. Like Titmuss, Crosland believed that greater equality should be the central goal, and that it could be achieved most effectively through an expansion of public services. Crosland, however, did not share the moralism of Titmuss and Tawney. He did not believe that it was possible to distinguish as clearly as they did between 'what was right and what was wrong'. As Raymond Plant has written, he saw 'moral outlook' as a 'matter of personal commitment and emotional predilection':

> This meant that there could be no decisive arguments for a particular set of political values, including his own. Given that he wanted to pursue an egalitarian strategy, he had to accept that this was a personal preference and this had an important bearing on his political strategy.
>
> (Plant 1996: 172)

Furthermore, Crosland believed that people were more self-interested and less inclined to altruism than Titmuss supposed. In Crosland's view, people's 'value preferences had to be taken as given' and there was little point in trying to create a moral consensus as Titmuss or (especially) Tawney sought to do. Instead, he tried to sidestep this lack of consensus. He argued that the proceeds of economic growth would make it possible to redistribute in favour of the poor without antagonizing the majority of voters who were not poor. Everyone would be getting better off, but the poor would be getting better off more quickly. Public services such as health, education and welfare were especially valuable in this regard, since they were of particular benefit to the poor while still used by everyone else. This made it possible to improve the relative position of the poor while avoiding a 'direct challenge to substantial numbers of citizens who may not share egalitarian values but who would also benefit from increased public provision' (Plant 1996: 175). As David Marquand (1996: 24) has pointed out, Crosland's was a technical rather than a moral case for equality. It demanded redistribution but offered 'no convincing moral argument for doing so'.

A third factor that shaped the quasi-Titmuss paradigm was the upsurge in unemployment from the mid-1970s. This seemed to exemplify the futility of trying to solve social problems by changing people. Why worry about the motivation of the unemployed when there were not enough jobs for them anyway? As the Supplementary Benefits Commission itself noted in 1980, increasing incentives 'while unemployment accelerates upwards is like trying to encourage somebody to jump into a swimming pool while the water is drained out' (SBC 1980: 41).

The fourth and perhaps the most important influence upon the Quasi-Titmuss paradigm was the growth of inequality in Britain in the late 1970s and 1980s. The conceptualization and measurement of income inequality have been much debated. Much depends, for example, upon whether the assessment is based on the income or expenditure of households and on whether or not the self-employed are included. Even when all possible qualifications have been made, however, there is still no doubt that the gap between the richest and poorest households widened at a rate that was probably unprecedented in British history, and which was matched in no other developed country (Goodman *et al.* 1997; Hills 1998). Moreover, the widening differences in living standards were mirrored in growing inequalities in health (Townsend *et al.* 1988; Wilkinson 1989). It was this growth in inequality and the concomitant rise in relative poverty that did more than anything else to reinforce the hostility of the quasi-Titmuss paradigm to attempts to locate the causes of poverty in the behaviour and attitudes of the poor themselves.

This hostility was exemplified in the debate about transmitted deprivation that followed a speech by the then Secretary of State for Social Services, Sir Keith Joseph. Speaking in 1972, Joseph suggested that 'much deprivation and maladjustment' might be transmitted from one generation to another through family attitudes or poor parenting. He pointed to a 'cycle of deprivation' through which parents 'who were themselves deprived in one or more ways in childhood, become the parents of another generation of deprived children'. The speech provoked uproar, but Joseph was still able to initiate a Joint Working Party into Transmitted Deprivation (JWPTD), composed of civil servants and prominent academics and researchers. This led in turn to the launch of a seven-year programme of research funded by Joseph's department and administered by the JWPTD.

As the final report on the programme noted, the initial expectation was that the research would focus 'on a minority of severely and multiply deprived families whose various problems . . . appeared to be perpetuated across generations by their processes of child-rearing' (Brown and Madge 1982: 3). Some of the studies funded by the programme did retain the original focus upon the most disadvantaged families. In general these studies provided 'mixed support' for the cycle of deprivation thesis. There was evidence of significant continuities across the generations, but also 'many exceptions to this pattern' (Madge 1983: 197–8). It was not clear why some individuals and families were able to buck the trend and others were not. A review of the existing evidence conducted at the outset of the programme concluded that 'we delude ourselves if we think that nothing short of massive social change can influence cycles of disadvantage.' The 'challenge for the future', it concluded, was to discover 'how we can bring about discontinuities in cycles of disadvantage' (Rutter and Madge 1976: 327).

In fact, however, this 'challenge' was not taken up and the 'whole scope of the programme' was subsequently 'altered' following discussions within the Joint Working Party. There was 'an emphatic shift in the programme's concern', and 'it moved away from the narrow problem family focus to discuss the evidence for the existence and transmission of a wide range of disadvantaging circumstances' (Brown and Madge 1982: 10). This led 'inevitably' to the conclusion that 'disadvantage is deeply rooted in the structure of our society'. It led also to explanations 'not only of poverty but even of poor health or child abuse' that emphasized 'the importance of the uneven distribution of income and wealth, of the unequal structure of employment, of the class-related pattern of life chances in terms of morbidity, educational achievement and even personal happiness' (pp. 5–6).

This episode is significant because it illustrates the ways in which the domination of the quasi-Titmuss paradigm served to inhibit discussion of some issues and questions. The effect was to create something akin to an intellectual void. At the same time, however, new arguments were being formulated – and very old ones refashioned – that were to fill this void and restore these issues to the centre of the welfare debate. In order to explain how this came about it is necessary to look briefly at the American welfare debate in the 1960s and 1970s.

Blaming the victim? Welfare and egalitarianism in the USA in the 1960s and 1970s

A similar void had developed in the USA, where the welfare debate had come to be dominated by what is termed here the American egalitarian perspective.

The first point to make is that in the 1960s and 1970s the American debate about welfare was inextricably linked to that about race. Although the civil rights legislation had granted formal equality to black Americans, it had done nothing in the immediate term to remove the legacy of past discrimination and deprivation. African and Hispanic Americans in particular were far more likely to experience poverty and to be on welfare. Moreover, the lack of education and training opportunities in the past meant that they were ill-equipped to take advantage of a booming economy and the prohibition of formal discrimination.

It was these barriers that the War on Poverty and other Great Society programmes were intended to remove. These included the liberalization of welfare – discussed in Chapter 2 – along with an array of education, health care, public housing and work programmes. All were designed to compensate the poor, and especially the black poor, for the injustices of the past and to enable them to participate fully in American life. In 1965, however, a report produced within the US Department of Labor had called for a more radical restructuring of the US welfare state. It proposed the introduction of family allowances for all children, and far more comprehensive jobs and training programmes. As Steve Teles (1996: 82) has noted, its recommendations constituted a 'system of social insurance for all families' that would target resources on poor black families within a universalist framework. In the light of this it is perhaps not surprising that Titmuss sent a personal note of support to the prime architect of the plan, Daniel P. Moynihan (Welshman n.d.). What may be more surprising is that far from being welcomed by many on the American left, the report was denounced for encouraging a 'new form of subtle racism' that explained racial inequalities by the 'weaknesses and defects of the Negro himself' (Ryan 1967: 458).

The report provoked this reaction because it justified its proposals in terms of the need to avert the imminent collapse of the black family. In essence it argued that the fact that welfare was paid only to lone mothers created a financial incentive for the formation of one-parent families. This was all the more important, since high unemployment among black men had stripped them of their role as breadwinners. The case for family allowances, then, was that they would lessen this discrimination against two-parent families. Similarly, the case for work programmes was that they would restore the economic status and self-esteem of black men.

The report, however, did not stop there. It went on to suggest that the black family was particularly vulnerable because of 'cultural weaknesses' that were rooted in slavery. The slave owners had deliberately broken up families, and this meant that the mother–child union was a more significant family form in black culture than it was among whites. In what became a notorious phrase, the report referred to the black family being pushed into 'a tangle of pathology' by 'the incredible mistreatment to which it has been subjected over the past three centuries' (Rainwater and Yancey 1967: 75). To support this claim, the report presented a battery of statistics on out-of-wedlock births, drug misuse, delinquency and underachievement in education. It was this candid discussion of problem behaviours among poor black communities that made the Moynihan Report so controversial, and made the debate that it provoked a watershed in the politics of welfare in the USA.

One of the report's fiercest critics was William Ryan, a professor of psychology and prominent civil rights activist. Ryan argued that Moynihan drew 'dangerous and inexact conclusions from weak and insufficient data'. It was simply wrong to attribute the allegedly high 'illegitimacy' rate among black Americans to 'Negro family stability as a sub-cultural trait'. The difference between the rates for whites and blacks were due to differences in access to abortion and contraception, and to the fact that whites were less likely to report 'illegitimate' births and more likely to form 'shotgun marriages'. The real explanation, then, was 'a systematic inequality of access to a variety of services and information' (Ryan 1967: 459).

Moynihan and Ryan continued to argue over the data for years, and both were to claim that they were vindicated by subsequent events (Ryan 1976: 312; Moynihan 1997: 181). Much more significant here, however, was Ryan's assault on Moynihan's explanation of the social problems of poor black communities as the product of past oppression. In effect, argued Ryan, liberals such as Moynihan were having it both ways. They proclaimed that all people were equal, but then argued that black people were disproportionately likely to behave in dysfunctional or unsociable ways because of what white people had done to them in the past. This, said Ryan, was 'an ingenious way of "coping a plea"'. Liberal America was pleading guilty to the oppression 'against the Negro that happened 100 years ago, in order to escape trial for the crimes of today' (Ryan 1967: 464).

Ryan subsequently widened the scope of his critique in a brilliantly written and highly influential book, *Blaming the Victim*. In this, Ryan castigated a 'new ideology' that attributed 'defect and inadequacy to the malignant nature of poverty, injustice, slum life, and racial difficulties' (Ryan 1976: 7). For all its talk of past injustice and inequalities, this approach still insisted that the victim of those injustices had to change too. 'He is at fault, although through no fault of his own' (p. 84). Ryan explained this perverse reasoning in 'psychological terms'. It was, he said, the result of a subconscious process of 'reconciliation' that allowed the self-professed liberal to satisfy 'both his self-interest and his charitable concerns' (p. 27).

There were, then, two aspects of Ryan's argument that were distinctive and important. First, he insisted that there was nothing deviant or pathological about the behaviours and attitudes of the people who lived in poor black communities. Second, he claimed that those who argued otherwise were guilty of reinforcing racist stereotypes. For Ryan, the concentration of social problems within poor black communities was due entirely to social and economic inequalities, and to racist institutions and practices. To suggest otherwise was to fail to recognize the ways in which inequalities impacted upon the lives of the poor, and the so-called liberals who eased their consciences by talking about 'environmental causation' were part of the problem, not part of the solution.

It is argued here that this represents a third perspective on welfare, one that can reasonably be termed American egalitarianism. It is a perspective that takes one stage further the emphasis upon structure and the denial of agency that characterized the quasi-Titmuss paradigm. It sees the role of welfare as to contribute to a process of giving back to black Americans 'what we took away'.

> For the millions of grown and half-grown Negro Americans who have already been damaged, we must make up for the injury that we did to them. This is what we must compensate for; not for some supposed inherent or acquired inferiority or weakness or instability of the victim whom we injured.
>
> (Ryan 1967: 466)

This perspective was shared by many other writers and activists, and the anger directed at Moynihan was to have a profound impact upon public discussions of poverty and welfare. In the first half of the 1960s, sociologists such as Kenneth Clark and Lee Rainwater had indeed argued that the circumstances into which 'so many disadvantaged blacks are born' produced 'modes of adaptation' and created 'norms and patterns of behaviour that take the form of a self-perpetuating pathology' (Wilson 1987: 4). Even

Michael Harrington, whose *The Other America* – first published in 1962 – remains the classic study of poverty in America, had written of a 'personality of poverty, a type of human being produced by the grinding, wearing life of the slums' (Harrington 1997: 122).

Discussion of these issues, however, was heavily circumscribed in the wake of the criticisms levelled at Moynihan. As William Julius Wilson (1987: 4) has written, these 'had the effect of curtailing serious research on minority problems in the inner city for over a decade, as liberal scholars shied away from researching behaviour construed as unflattering or stigmatizing to particular racial minorities.' The critical point for Wilson was that this meant that those scholars were 'confused and defensive' when they were forced to readdress 'the problems of inner-city social dislocations' in the 1980s. Furthermore, there was another reason why they were so defensive: the War on Poverty seemed to be failing. There had been 'the most comprehensive civil rights legislation and the most comprehensive antipoverty programme in the nation's history'. This made it very difficult for the liberals who had championed those programmes to 'explain the sharp increase in inner-city poverty, joblessness, female-headed families, and welfare dependency since 1970 without reference to individual or group deficiencies' (Wilson 1987: 132).

Wilson's own analysis of the War on Poverty was that it had relied too heavily upon training and employment programmes and had paid too little attention to macroeconomic policy. The US economy was stagnating for much of the 1970s, and the decline in employment opportunities inevitably undermined the effectiveness and credibility of the programmes. Moreover, this was part of a general failure to incorporate those programmes within a broader strategy that benefited all Americans. 'I am convinced', Wilson wrote, 'that the problems of the truly disadvantaged will have to be attacked primarily through universal programs that enjoy the support and commitment of a broad constituency' (1987: 120).

Wilson's book *The Truly Disadvantaged* thus occupies a pivotal position in relation to the issues discussed in this chapter. On the one hand, his critique of the War on Poverty echoed that of Titmuss himself. On the other hand, he pointed to the ways in which the 'liberal perspective' had become 'less persuasive and convincing' because of the reluctance of many liberal commentators to 'discuss openly or, in some instances, even to acknowledge the sharp increase in social pathologies in ghetto communities' (Wilson 1987: 6).

Conclusion

It is important to emphasize again the close links between the three perspectives discussed in this chapter. Members of the quasi-Titmuss school often cited Ryan (Sinfield 1978; Walker 1996), while Ryan (1976: 302) himself noted the 'strong resemblance' of his analysis to that of Titmuss. Nevertheless, the fact that these perspectives are all variations on a common theme does not mean that the variations are unimportant. The most important difference is, of course, that the importance that Titmuss attached to altruism meant that he did discuss agency. He did write about the ways in which welfare could shape attitudes and values, and did believe that this was one of its roles and purposes. It is this that distinguishes him from the quasi-Titmuss school and American egalitarians such as Ryan. As Williams *et al.* have noted,

> Certainly it is true that most mainstream welfare research of the 1960s and 1970s focused on the structural determinants of people's problems and that social inequalities were viewed deterministically and unidimensionally in terms of social class. With the possible exception of Titmuss's work on altruism . . . the notion of human agency was, by and large, ignored.
>
> (Williams *et al.* 1999: 11)

It is this neglect of agency within the quasi-Titmuss paradigm and its American counterpart that forms the context for much of what follows in this book. In William Julius Wilson's words, this neglect 'allowed conservative analysts to dominate the public discourse' on welfare 'throughout the first half of the 1980s' (Wilson 1997: 176). The most important of these 'conservative analysts' was Charles Murray, whose work is discussed in the next chapter.

Note

1 The term paradigm is customarily used to refer to a set of related ideas, and the term school to refer to the writers and commentators most closely associated with those ideas.

Further reading

Alcock *et al.* (2001) contains extracts from many of Titmuss's most important writings on welfare, and Oakley and Ashton (1997) is a reprint of *The Gift Relationship* with new commentaries. The best single book on Titmuss is still that by Reisman (1977), and the same author has also provided the best introduction to the ideas of Tawney (Reisman 1982). A recent book within the Titmuss tradition is that by Page (1996). The pivotal figure in the quasi-Titmuss paradigm is Peter Townsend, and the most important sources are his magisterial study of poverty (1979) and two earlier volumes of essays (1973, 1975). The most recent evidence on inequalities of income and wealth in Britain is reviewed in Goodman *et al.* (1997), Hills (1998) and Rowlingson *et al.* (1999). Inequalities in health are analysed by Shaw *et al.* (1999) and Wilkinson (1996). The debate around the Moynihan Report in the USA is documented in detail in Rainwater and Yancey (1967).

Welfare and self-interest

The perspective that is explored in this chapter starts from the assumption that the overwhelming majority of people will act rationally to better the conditions of themselves and their dependants. It follows from this that the objective of welfare should be to channel this desire for self-improvement in ways which promote the common good. At the heart of this perspective is the belief that the rules and regulations which govern entitlement to benefits and services must reward those activities and attributes which should be encouraged and penalize those which need to be discouraged. If they do not do this then they will lead people to behave in ways which damage themselves and the communities in which they live.

The argument that welfare does indeed generate such 'perverse incentives' is associated most closely with the American conservative Charles Murray. Murray's writings on welfare are examined in this chapter, along with those of the British politician Frank Field.

At first sight the differences between Frank Field's position and that of Charles Murray could scarcely be greater. Whereas Field has sought to restructure welfare provision, Murray would end it for large numbers of poor people. Charles Murray describes himself as an 'authentic radical' whose vision of a severely curtailed role for government in welfare places him firmly 'outside the mainstream of politics'. He does not put forward a list of 'incremental, politically practicable reforms' for the simple reason that he cannot think of any that would do any good (Murray 1996: 91). In contrast, Frank Field has been at the forefront of welfare politics in Britain for 30 years, as a writer, lobbyist and MP, and as Minister for Welfare Reform during the first 15 months of the Blair government. Far from eschewing the details of policy, he has produced blueprints for the reform of almost every facet of the social security system.

These differences are real and important but they are not the whole story.

There are also striking similarities in the ways in which Murray and Field think about welfare. First, they both believe that self-interest is, in Field's words, 'the great driving force in each of us' and 'always will be the greatest (but not the only) engine force for social advance' (Field 1998: 19). Second, they both believe that the way in which welfare is provided and regulated exerts a decisive influence upon the attitudes and behaviour of those who receive it. The first step in resolving any welfare issue is to ask: how do things appear to those affected? What behaviour is being encouraged and rewarded? What is being discouraged and penalized? How far are these 'signals' buttressed by tangible incentives and sanctions? Third, they have both been heavily influenced by their perception of how welfare actually operates 'on the ground'. In Field's case that 'ground' has been his parliamentary constituency of Birkenhead, and many of his ideas have been shaped by the comments and activities of his constituents. In Murray's case the 'ground' has been somewhat more far-flung: the cities of the USA and the villages of Thailand.

Charles Murray

Like many of the writers discussed in this book, Charles Murray has had an unorthodox career, and it is impossible to locate his ideas within conventional academic boundaries.[1] He studied Russian politics at Harvard and worked for six years in Thailand, first as a volunteer with the Peace Corps and then for the United States Agency for International Development on a project examining the local impact of development aid. Returning to the United States in the mid-1970s, he worked on a series of evaluations of Great Society programmes. He became increasingly sceptical of the effectiveness of such programmes and in 1982 wrote the pamphlet *Safety Nets and the Truly Needy* for a prominent conservative think tank, the Heritage Foundation. This argued that the abolition of the poverty programmes would help the poor more than it would harm them, and brought Murray to the attention of William Hammett, the president of another conservative think tank, the Manhattan Institute. Hammett offered Murray the opportunity to develop his ideas on welfare: a two-year research fellowship at the Institute, together with research assistance and other support.

An early article by Murray in the journal *The Public Interest* was relatively circumspect. It noted that the huge sums spent on the federal War on Poverty since the mid-1960s had failed to reduce poverty, and that this had fuelled demands for drastic cuts in social welfare budgets. Murray argued that the failure to reduce poverty was due in large part to two other changes which had occurred at the time that the War on Poverty was being fought. These were the decline in the 'husband–wife family' and the drop in work levels among the poor. He acknowledged that there were 'other reasons as well – the large proportion of the social welfare budget spent on people above the poverty level being perhaps the most notable' (Murray 1982: 16). Nevertheless, he concluded that

> It is genuinely an open issue – intellectually as well as politically – whether we should be talking about spending cuts, or whether we should be considering an overhaul of the entire welfare system as conceived in the Great Society.
>
> (p. 16)

Two years later Murray published *Losing Ground*, and by this time that 'genuinely open issue' had been resolved most emphatically. As Steve Teles (1996: 148) has observed, there 'is no way to overestimate the effect' that the book had upon 'the intellectual debate on poverty' in the USA. It shifted the focus and transformed the tone of that debate, and had an important if less direct impact in Britain.

There were two components of the case which Charles Murray presented in *Losing Ground*. The first was an assertion about data, a statement about trends in poverty and other indicators of social pathology. The second was his interpretation of those data, his explanation of those trends. In consequence the book gave rise to two parallel but discrete debates: one about the accuracy and validity of the evidence Murray provided and the other about the plausibility of his analyses of whatever changes had occurred.

These debates are discussed here in some detail because they raise issues which recur throughout this part of the book. The discussion can most conveniently be divided into three parts; the arguments originally presented in *Losing Ground*, the debate generated by those arguments, and the subsequent shift in Murray's position. Before proceeding to any of this, however, there are three preliminary points which must be made.

The first point is that *Losing Ground* said nothing about the costs of welfare. Nowhere in the book did Murray discuss the levels of taxation required to fund welfare programmes or the burden which this imposed upon the wider economy. His focus was simply and solely upon the impact of welfare upon behaviour. The second point is that the subtitle of *Losing Ground* is misleading. The book is not about *American Social Policy 1950–1980*. It is about welfare narrowly defined. Virtually all of Murray's evidence relates to AFDC and to food stamps for the non-disabled and non-elderly – even though they represented less than 8 per cent of all income transfers at the time when he was writing. The third point is that throughout the book Murray presents his data in a form which equates the black population of the USA with the poor and the white population with the non-poor. This is despite the fact that there were in 1980 some 19.7 million whites living beneath the poverty level and 1.4 million black households with an income well in excess of the poverty line. Indeed, a recurring theme of *Losing Ground* is the growing bifurcation of the black population into an increasingly successful middle class and an underclass mired in poverty and dependency.

Murray's explanation for presenting the data in this form was that it was the only way in which he could demonstrate trends over time. Strictly speaking, this required a longitudinal survey – one which tracked the incomes and other circumstances of the same individuals from one year to another.[2] No such longitudinal data were available.

> But we do know that blacks in the United States, besides being vulnerable to outright racial discrimination, are disproportionately poor and disproportionately disadvantaged in educational background, economic status and social status. We may take advantage of this situation to use the statistics for blacks in the United States as the best-available proxy for the longitudinal sample of 'disadvantaged Americans' that would be preferable.
>
> (Murray 1984: 54)

Statistics in the United States are routinely broken down by race. Nevertheless, it was noted in Chapter 1 that race plays an important and sensitive role in welfare politics in the USA, and Murray's equation of 'black' with 'poor' was especially contentious given his focus upon the importance of behaviour as a cause of poverty.

Losing Ground: the data

The cornerstone of Murray's argument was that the number of people living below the official poverty line fell consistently between 1950 and the late 1960s, but then remained constant – or even rose slightly – during the 1970s. Federal spending on the poor had soared between 1968 and 1980, yet, 'perversely, poverty chose those years to halt a decline that had been underway for two decades' (Murray 1984: 58).

For Murray the 'most damning of the statistics' was the growth in what he termed 'latent poverty'. By this he meant not only the numbers living below the official poverty line but also 'those who are above the poverty line in the official measure only by virtue of government support' (p. 64). The 'latent poor', in other words, were people of working age who were unable to make a sufficient living on their own and hence dependent upon welfare to keep out of poverty. It was the size of this group which constituted the real measure of success or failure, since 'economic independence – standing on one's own abilities and accomplishments – is of paramount importance in determining the quality of a family's life' (p. 65).

Latent poverty had fallen from around one-third of the US population in 1950 to just over 18 per cent in 1968, but had then steadied before rising again to 22 per cent in 1980. Murray claimed that the cause of this 'extraordinary' trend lay in the two factors highlighted in his earlier article: the collapse of the family, and especially the black family; and the withdrawal from the labour force of young men, especially young black men.

It is very important to be clear about what had happened to the structure of the family if Murray's arguments are to be properly understood. The key was the change in the relative birth rates of married and unmarried women. The overall birth rate had nearly halved between 1960 and 1980, from 118 births per 1,000 women aged 15–44 to 68 per 1,000 women. This decline had occurred in almost every age group, among married and unmarried women, among white women and black women and among poor women and non-poor women. It had been greater, however, among married women and especially married black women, and most of all among very young black married women. The outcome was that although the number of what Murray termed 'illegitimate births' fell, those births were still a higher proportion of the total because the number of 'legitimate births' was falling even faster.[3] For Murray the most important figure was the 'illegitimacy rate' – 'illegitimate births not as a rate per 1,000 women but as a percentage of all births' (p. 126).

Thus defined, the 'illegitimacy' rate had risen sharply, and especially for black women. Between 1950 and 1980 births to single women had risen from 17 per cent of the total to 48 per cent of the total among black women and from 2 to 11 per cent among white women (pp. 126–7). The rise was sharpest of all among teenage black women, and by 1980, 82 per cent of all births to black women aged 15–19 were 'illegitimate'. The outcome of all this was a dramatic increase in the proportion of black families headed by a single mother and in the proportion of children being raised in such families. Put the other way around, the proportion of black families which consisted of husband–wife households declined from 78 per cent in 1950 to 72 per cent in 1968 and then fell by a further 13 percentage points to 59 per cent in 1980. By comparison, the proportion among white families had fallen by only 3 percentage points over the whole 30-year period, from 88 per cent in 1950 to 85 per cent in 1980. This, then, was the collapse of the black family, which, Murray claimed, had now gone beyond anything envisaged in the Moynihan Report.

The most crucial point of all, however, was that there was a clear cohort effect. Not only did the birth rate of married women drop more than for single women, but it dropped much faster among older single women than among those under 25. Indeed, between 1965 and 1970 the number of births per 1,000 women actually increased among single women aged 15–19, while it was dropping among older single women and married women of all ages. This was true of both black and white women. Irrespective of race, it was the youngest age group that bucked the trend towards fewer births. 'For this narrow population of women, something overrode the broad social (and medical) trends that produced falling birth rates among everyone else' (Murray 1984: 128). Murray went on to argue that this cohort effect was equally marked in respect of the labour market. He compared the average unemployment rate for black males between 1955 and 1965 with the average for 1966–80. For the older age groups the rate was lower in the second period; for the younger age groups it was higher.

> During the same fifteen-year period in which every black male age group at or above the age of 25 experienced decreased unemployment compared with the preceding fifteen years, every group under the age of 25 showed a major increase in unemployment.
>
> (Murray 1984: 73–4)

More striking still were the data on the Labour Force Participation (LFP) rate of black males. The LFP rate is a measure of the proportion of the total population that is either working or unemployed. A decline in LFP thus represents an increase in the proportion of the relevant population that has effectively dropped out of the labour force, neither being in legal employment nor looking for it. According to Murray's statistics this is exactly what occurred among black males but not among their white counterparts. The differential between the LFP rate for blacks and whites began to increase among the youngest age groups in the mid-1960s, and the gap then widened among the older age groups in subsequent years. It was, said Murray, 'as if contagion were spreading slowly upward from young to old'.

> What was really happening, of course, is that the same people were getting older . . . We are watching a generational phenomenon. For whatever reasons, black males born in the early 1950s and thereafter had a different posture towards the labour market from their fathers and older brothers.
>
> (Murray 1984: 81)

The abruptness and scale of the changes in illegitimacy rates and LFP rates among blacks made them 'demographic wonder(s), without precedent in the American experience' (p. 130).

Losing Ground: the explanation

Thus far Murray had established that the rise in latent poverty was due primarily to the rise in family breakdown and decline in work levels which had occurred among the poor. These trends had in turn been traced to a shift in behaviour on the part of the poor that had first become evident in the youngest age groups in the mid-1960s. The clinching argument as far as Murray was concerned was this was the cohort that had reached adulthood and entered the labour market just as the War on Poverty was beginning. It was this cohort that had been exposed to the new welfare regime at the most formative stage of their lives.

The most compelling explanation for the marked shift in the fortunes of the poor is that they continued to respond, as they always had, to the world as they found it, but that we – meaning the not-poor and un-disadvantaged – had changed the rules of their world.

(Murray 1984: 9)

Murray's experiences in Thailand had made him aware that behaviour which seemed rational to government planners often made no sense what-soever to people living in the rural villages. The same gulf existed between the American poor and the policy-makers in Washington. Those who planned the War on Poverty failed to recognize that 'the behaviors that are "rational" are different at different economic levels'.

I begin with the proposition that all, poor and non-poor alike, use the same general calculus in arriving at decisions; only the exigencies are different. Poor people play with fewer chips and cannot wait as long for results. Therefore they tend to reach decisions that a more affluent person would not reach.

(Murray 1984: 155)

Nothing illustrated this better than the consequences of the surge in the numbers in receipt of AFDC benefits, from some four million in 1966 to around 11 million in 1973. The numbers on welfare did not increase because more people became eligible for the programme, but because more people who were entitled to claim did so. One estimate – not cited by Murray – is that take-up rose from 42 per cent in 1967 to 64 per cent in 1970 and to 87 per cent in 1973 (Teles 1996: 20). The sharply higher levels of take-up reflected the change in the attitudes of claimants towards welfare that occurred during the War on Poverty. AFDC was much more attractive to claimants in the early 1970s than it had been a decade earlier because the levels of benefit were more generous and – more importantly – because the tone and manner of the administration of the programme had been trans-formed.

The details of the changes are less important here than the inferences which Murray drew. The rise in the welfare caseload was the aggregate result of the decisions of millions of individuals that their self-interest was now best served by claiming benefits. This, of course, was precisely what the policy makers had expected and intended to happen when they relaxed the rules. What they had not anticipated was that this expansion of welfare would in turn fuel an upsurge in 'illegitimate births' and the withdrawal of many poor youths from the formal labour market. To illustrate how this occurred Murray created 'Harold and Phyllis'.

In Murray's vignette, Harold and Phyllis are a young couple who have to decide what to do now that Phyllis has become pregnant. Should they marry? Should Phyllis go on welfare? Should Harold take the low-paid job that he finds unattractive but which is the only one available? Murray claims that in 1960 the couple would have been better off if they had married and Harold worked full time. By 1970, however, the financial incentives were reversed. They would not marry. Instead, Phyllis would claim AFDC while cohabiting with Harold, who would supplement her welfare cheque with occasional part-time work (Murray 1984: 156–62).

Murray emphasized that Harold and Phyllis had not changed their character or values between 1960 and 1970. They had not suddenly become 'welfare bums'. It was, he said, a matter of 'dollars and cents' (p. 160), and of Harold and Phyllis taking those steps which maximized their quality of life.

> There is no 'breakdown of the work ethic' in this account of rational choices among alternatives . . . There is no need to invoke the specters of cultural pathology or inferior upbringing. The choices may be seen much more simply, much more naturally, as the behavior of people responding to the reality of the world around them.
>
> (Murray 1984: 162)

The impact of the Great Society programmes, however, was not just a matter of financial incentives. They also transformed the 'incentives associated with status' (p. 177).

The deliberate eradication of any sense of stigma from claiming welfare had inevitably served to diminish the relative status that had previously been enjoyed by those who maintained themselves and their dependants, often through unpleasant and ill-paid work. If even persistent unemployment was the fault of the system and not of the individual, then there was no longer any basis for blaming those who failed to work or praising those who did work. The result was what Murray termed the 'homogenization' of the poor: 'all must be victims. They were not permitted to be superior to one another' (p. 181). Once again, this was what the policy-makers had expected and intended. Distinctions between the deserving and the undeserving poor had no place in the society they were trying to create. From Murray's perspective, however, the refusal to hold anyone responsible for his or her failures was catastrophic. The only way in which people could escape from poverty was to hold down a steady job and to postpone children until they could be provided for. The 'homogenization of the poor', however, removed the status which had hitherto reinforced such behaviour, especially in the eyes of the young.

> To someone who is not yet persuaded of the satisfactions of making one's own way, there is something laughable about a person who doggedly keeps working at a lousy job for no tangible reason at all. And when working no longer provides either income or status, the last reason for working has truly vanished. The man who keeps on working is, in fact, a chump.
>
> (Murray 1984: 185)

The effects of the 'Great Society' programmes, then, were to belittle and undermine the very behaviours which should have been encouraged and rewarded. Instead of providing ladders out of poverty they had 'inadvertently built a trap' (p. 9).

It is this question of stigma that illustrates most clearly the gulf which separates Murray's view of human nature from that of Titmuss. It was seen in Chapter 1 that Titmuss saw the removal of stigma as the hallmark of a successful social policy; one which was able both to redistribute resources and to foster altruism and a sense of social cohesion. For Murray the removal of stigma and the moral judgements which it embodied threatened the basis of a responsible civil society. As he argued in a later book, it was the duty of governments to 'provide an enviroment in which people accept responsibility for their actions'. 'An acceptable social policy', then, is 'one that validates the individual's responsibility for the consequences of his behaviour'. This sense of responsibility had to be authentic. It could not be faked by policies which tried to create an impression that people were self-reliant, while in reality protecting them from the consequences of their own actions. 'Or to put it another way, a social policy that induces people to believe that they are not responsible for their lives is one that inhibits the pursuit of happiness and is to that extent immoral' (Murray 1988: 131). From Murray's perspective the structural inequalities which so preoccupied Titmuss and other writers discussed in Chapter 1 were real, but they were also beside the point. 'People – all people, black or white, rich or poor – may be unequally responsible for what has happened to them in the past, but all are equally responsible for what they do next' (Murray 1984: 234).

The policy implications which Murray drew from his analysis were simple and bleak. If the behaviours which created poverty were a rational response to the existing rules, then those rules would have to change. If it were possible he would favour the 'Alexandrian solution: cut the knot for there is no way to untie it' (p. 228). This would require the elimination of public welfare for the non-disabled of working age, save for the short-term unemployment insurance programme and a residue of highly discretionary local schemes. In 1984 such a degree of change seemed impossible, but it will be seen in Chapter 6 that the impact of *Losing Ground* was itself to help to change what was and what was not 'politically feasible'. The important point to stress here, however, is that Murray was not seeking to abolish welfare in order to reduce the budget, to combat fraud or to create the scope for tax cuts. The rationale was solely that to do so would 'radically' improve the lives of 'large numbers of poor people' (p. 229).

Losing Ground: first critics

The remarkable impact of *Losing Ground* owed much to the skill – and expense – with which it was published and marketed. The Manhattan

Institute sent over 700 complimentary copies to journalists in press and television, public officials and politicians (including Conservative ministers in Britain). The Institute was able to ensure that Murray was able to meet personally a wide range of opinion formers, and it also funded an extensive speaking tour of the USA (Lane 1985). *The Sunday Times* was later to pay for Murray to spend a month in Britain writing a series of articles on the spread of the underclass across the Atlantic (De Parle 1994). All of this meant that *Losing Ground* reached an audience far wider than that of any conventional academic book.

The response of most academics in the USA to Murray's arguments was a combination of shock, dismay and – especially – anger. Many of the early critics of *Losing Ground* focused upon its claim that latent poverty had risen despite the growth in welfare spending. It will be remembered that Murray defined latent poverty as the number of people unable to keep themselves out of poverty before receiving governmental transfers. Sheldon Danziger and Peter Gottschalk retorted that if it was defined in this way latent poverty was bound to grow in any period in which market incomes were falling, either because real wages were declining or because unemployment was rising. Furthermore, they argued that Murray's comparison of the poverty rates among white and black households was misleading because he failed to acknowledge that poverty fell by nearly half among black households with male heads between 1967 and 1980. The reason why black households as a whole lost ground to white households was that they were increasingly likely to be headed by a woman (Danziger and Gottschalk 1985: 3).

This kind of argument, however, simply raised in a different form the question of what was causing what. Murray would never be swayed by claims that welfare programmes were having to contend with growing problems of unemployment or lone parenthood because he started from the presumption that it was welfare which was causing these problems in the first place.

Much more telling was Robert Greenstein's (1985: 12) accusation that Murray was guilty of 'deceptive numbers juggling'. Greenstein pointed out that Murray's figures related only to one atypical state – Pennsylvania – and that he ignored developments before 1970 that 'undermined his case'. The real value of welfare benefits had fallen by almost one-third between 1970 and 1980 but the number of female-headed households had continued to rise.

This latter point was taken up by David Ellwood and Lawrence Summers (1986). They claimed that the number of black children on AFDC fell by 5 per cent between 1972 and 1980, but the number of black children in female-headed households still increased by 20 per cent over the same period. Ellwood and Summers conceded that people may have ceased to respond to changes in benefit levels once a threshold had been reached. 'But', they added, 'we can think of no story crediting AFDC with a very large part in inducing changed family structures which is consistent with a falling absolute number of children on the program' (Ellwood and Summers 1986: 69). Equally striking was Murray's failure to mention that the birth rate for unmarried black women fell by 13 per cent during the 1970s, while that for unmarried white women rose by 27 per cent. This made it difficult to argue that AFDC was a major influence on unmarried births (Ellwood and Summers 1986: 69). Finally, Ellwood and Summers agreed that the labour market situation of young black men was 'bad and getting worse' (p. 73). This was not to say, however, that welfare was necessarily to blame. Very few young men were eligible for assistance in the first place, and so they would not have been affected directly by the expansion of the programmes.

Murray's response to criticisms such as these was to change the whole basis of his argument. In *Losing Ground* he had assumed that the poor 'reacted to economic incentives' just like other 'consumers' (Murray 1984: 291). Two years later, however, the focus had switched from the ways in which welfare generated perverse incentives to the ways in which it acted as an 'enabler'. 'Welfare', he now claimed, 'does not bribe poor women to have babies, it enables them to do so'.

> For the young woman who is not pregnant, enabling means that she does not ask, 'Do I want a welfare cheque badly enough to get pregnant?' but rather, 'If I happen to get pregnant, will the consequences really be so bad?'
>
> (Murray 1986a: 4)

What mattered, then, was not the precise level of welfare but whether or not it provided an income that was broadly sufficient to allow people to do what they naturally wanted to do. As Ellwood and Summers had anticipated, the critical notion had become that of the threshold. Once benefits were perceived as enough to enable the behaviour, then fluctuations above that level would have little or no effect.

Murray also changed his position in respect of the indirect effects of welfare upon the behaviour of the poor. In *Losing Ground* he had said that it 'is questionable whether social policy in a free society can create values that broadly affect behaviour' (Murray 1984: 295). In later writings, however, he began to argue that the 'perverse incentives' generated by the benefit system created new patterns of behaviour, which then became self-perpetuating. The mechanisms through which this happened were changes in the 'values and expectations of male behaviour' held within low-income communities. These in turn impacted upon the 'behaviour of men and women who never touch an AFDC cheque' (Murray 1986a: 7).

More striking still was Murray's new emphasis upon the importance of personal character and of the spirit of the times, the *Zeitgeist*. In an important article in 1985 James Q. Wilson had criticized Murray for rejecting 'the notion that character, the *Zeitgeist*, or cultural differences are necessary to an explanation' of welfare dependency (Wilson 1985: 9). Wilson argued that Murray had accepted too readily the assumption often made by economists that values and beliefs can be taken as given and that all that matters is the way in which people responded to changes in incentives. A year later Murray himself claimed that the importance of welfare reforms of the 1960s lay not only in 'changes in incentives and status rewards, but also . . . [in] a larger effect on the formation of character among poor young people, and especially black young poor people' (Murray 1986a: 9).

The exchange with James Q. Wilson illustrates Murray's remarkable facility for adopting opposing arguments as his own, and putting forward as an elaboration of his case points which had originally been made as a qualification of it. There was, however, to be one further shift in Murray's position, and this time it was to distance him still further from his critics. By the early 1990s he had begun to argue that it was 'illegitimacy' that was of overwhelming importance in understanding the growth of the underclass. In what became an infamous article in the *Wall Street Journal* he claimed that 'illegitimacy is the single most important social problem of our time' because 'it drives everything else' (Murray 1993). He later told a British audience: 'Communities in which large proportions of the children are born without fathers end up with enormous social problems. The "kicker" to this point of view was that this is true whether or not the mothers are working' (Murray 1998: 61). This was a direct challenge to the growing preoccupation of policy makers on both sides of the Atlantic with the work levels of the poor, a preoccupation which was itself a reflection of the influence of the perspective that is outlined in the next chapter. The debate between these perspectives is explored further in that chapter. What needs to be emphasized here is the enormous impact that Murray's earlier writings had upon the welfare debates in Britain and America. It is no exaggeration to say that Murray changed the focus of those debates. He did not ask what welfare costs, but how welfare affects behaviour. As Lawrence Mead has observed, '*Losing Ground* marks a sea change in the style of research and argument about poverty' (Mead 1988b: 23).

Frank Field

It was emphasized in the opening chapter of this book that there are very few writers on social policy whose ideas have not changed or developed over time. This is especially true of Frank Field. If it is the case that he entered the New Labour government having 'written more books than most of his colleagues had read' (Nye 1998: vii), then it is also the case that those books had not all said the same thing.

Frank Field first came to prominence when one of his earliest acts as Director of the Child Poverty Action Group was to draft a memorandum which argued that 'the poor had got poorer' under the Labour governments of 1964–70 (McCarthy 1986). He was to remain at CPAG until elected to Parliament in 1979, and after 1974 was also Director of the Low Pay Unit. As both lobbyist and politician he wrote extensively on social and economic policy in the 1970s and 1980s. Never happy to accept the constraints of party discipline, he was among the first to advocate the sale of council housing and his early writings on welfare anticipated some of the themes – and combative style – which were to become more pronounced in the 1990s. In 1971, for example, he co-authored the article which introduced the term the 'poverty trap' to describe the ways in which means tests penalize low-paid workers who manage to increase their earnings (Field and Piachaud 1971). More generally, he was always sceptical of any strategy that sought to aid the poor by appealing to the altruism or better nature of the more affluent taxpayers. Nevertheless, there was very little in these early writings about character or behaviour, and Field had not yet distanced himself from the quasi-Titmuss paradigm discussed in Chapter 1.

A significant influence upon the development of Field's ideas was his chairmanship of the House of Commons Select Committee on Social Security from 1990 to 1997. During these years the committee conducted inquiries into many facets of the benefits system. In particular it was the findings of the Commons committee that convinced Field that fraud and abuse were not inventions of the tabloid press or Conservative backwoodsmen, but were problems that Labour could not afford to ignore if it was to have any credibility with the electorate. The committee's work also enjoyed a high degree of cross-party support, and cemented Field's position as, in David Willets's phrase, 'many conservatives' favourite Labour politician' (Willets 1996: 31). This, of course, was unlikely to endear Field to many in his own party, but the transformation which followed the election of Tony Blair as leader in July 1994 gave Field an influence over Labour thinking which would have been inconceivable a few years earlier, and led eventually to his appointment as Minister for Welfare Reform in May 1997.

The development of New Labour's policies on welfare is examined in Chapter 7. The focus in this chapter is upon a series of books, essays and speeches by Field that began with *Making Welfare Work* in 1995 and continued beyond the general election of 1997. These are examined here because they set out a blueprint for welfare reform which shared Charles Murray's assumptions about the centrality and legitimacy of self-interest as a motive for human action, and the importance of welfare as an influence upon the behaviour of those who claim it. Field's position, however, differed from that of Murray in one crucial respect. In these writings he was seeking to restructure welfare, not to abolish it. This meant that the scope of his analysis was necessarily broader. Whereas Murray could take it as read that a majority of the American public would believe it to be in their own interest to cut back on the welfare paid to the poor, Field had to devise ways of securing popular support for the welfare reforms he was proposing. In his case, welfare had to channel the self-interest not just of the poor but of the electorate as well.

Making Welfare Work

Field's ideas about the role and purpose of welfare are rooted in what he describes as a 'Christian understanding of mankind'. We must start, he says, by accepting that we 'are less than perfect creatures'. This 'most fundamental aspect of each of us' means that 'unconditional altruism' can never be a 'realistic proposition for public as opposed to private conduct' (Field 1996: 109). It follows from this that the 'sanitised, post-Christian view of human character held by Titmuss' was 'built on sand' because the 'fallen side of mankind' was simply 'written out' of the script (Field 1997: 30–1). Writing during the general election campaign of 1997, Field claimed that what he called the 'Titmuss legacy' had 'immobilised Labour thinking' and established a 'post-war orthodoxy' that 'became an intellectual, political and moral cul-de-sac' (p. 31).

The first step in restructuring welfare, therefore, is for policy-makers to accept that people will pursue their self-interest. More than that, however, they must recognize that 'the shaping of certain types of character traits' is a 'proper goal for public policy' and that 'it is in the public interest to see certain aspects of character develop for their own sake' (Field 1996: 111). Welfare has a crucial role to play in this because it inevitably serves to punish some actions and to reward others. It is this conviction that the 'distribution of welfare is one of the great teaching forces open to advanced societies' (p. 111) that explains the ferocity with which Field attacked the growth of means testing. There was nothing that was novel about a politician on the centre left criticizing the means test. It was seen in Chapter 1 that a committment to universal benefits was central to the quasi-Titmuss paradigm. What made Field's contribution so distinctive was the grounds upon which he opposed means testing, and the way in which he used the language of Murray to denounce a policy instrument long favoured by conservative critics of the costs of state welfare.

Field argued that means tests penalize the behaviours which should be encouraged.

> Means-tested benefits, which are progressively withdrawn as income rises, act as a penalty on work and effort. Similarly, as savings can disqualify a person from benefit, means tests have a negative impact on savings levels.
>
> (Field 1997: 89)

Worse still, means tests reward the dishonesty of claimants who do not disclose an increase in their income. The result is that 'something in the order of half the country is now ensnared in means-tested welfare dependency. A welfare system increasingly shaped to concentrate help on the poor has turned out to have a monstrous effect on human motivation and honesty' (Field 1995: 92).

It follows that the solution is to create a benefits system which harnesses the self-interest of claimants so that they 'are motivated to leave the welfare roll, rather than, as at present, merely to maximise their income while remaining on welfare' (p. 76). *Making Welfare Work* proposed to do this by extending the coverage of insurance benefits which are not means-tested and so provide a platform from which claimants can move away from dependence on benefits by their own efforts. Field made much, for example, of the contrasting behaviour of households claiming insurance benefits because of unemployment or sickness and those in receipt of means-tested income support for the same reason. In the case of the latter, it was unusual for anyone else in the household to be in work since their earnings would be offset by reductions in benefit. If, on the other hand, 'a claimant is able to claim national insurance benefit, the likelihood is that his or her partner continues to work and therefore raises the household income above income support levels' (Field 1995: 149).

The strategy that Field developed in the mid-1990s, then, was to put whatever resources were available into a new insurance scheme that would replace means-tested provision. As he recognized, this would have involved some 'hard choices' regarding the current levels of benefits.

> Critics will point out that a policy of building up non-means-tested coverage at the expense of raising the real value of means-tested benefits will result in the very poorest gaining no help, and any increase in income going to those above the state minimum income level.
>
> (Field 1995: 77)

Field's response to such critics was that this was the price that had to be paid if the scope of the means test was to be curtailed. In any case, policies that focused solely on the poor have always failed in the past, and are unlikely to attract sufficient electoral support in the future. In the final analysis, he argued, the 'poor can only be protected by schemes which the better-off majority want to see prosper' (Field 1997: 19).

The problem, of course, is how to devise such a 'scheme'. How can the 'better-off majority' be persuaded that it is in their self-interest to support a benefits system which redistributes resources to the poor?

It will be seen in Chapter 7 that a central theme of 'New Labour' rhetoric on welfare is its insistence that the social exclusion of the poor can only be ended by making their inclusion worthwhile to those who will have to pay for it. Tony Blair in particular has sought to rebuild popular support for welfare by talking about the enlightened self-interest of the electorate and by presenting welfare reform as the basis of a new contract between government and governed.

The significance of *Making Welfare Work* was that it anticipated much of this approach and tried to map out a way in which it could be implemented. In order to achieve this, however, Field had to find a way of doing two things. First, he had to ensure that the better off made provision for such contingencies as old age and illness which was more adequate than that which they currently obtained through the state. They would be able to do this only by spreading their income more evenly over their lifetime – contributing enough when in work to fund their retirement and to provide cover against unemployment, illness or disability. As Field assumes that the better off will act rationally to further their own self-interest, he cannot expect them to make these contributions if they are being used to fund benefits for other people. At the same time, his second objective is to extend insurance to cover groups who are unable to pay contributions on their own behalf, and consequently will have to have those contributions paid for them.

Field attempted to square this circle by proposing what he termed 'stakeholder welfare'. 'Stakeholding' was already something of a buzz word in British politics in the mid-1990s, although the popularity of the term did not reflect any consistency in its usage. For Field, the defining characteristic of stakeholder welfare is that people own the welfare capital created by their contributions and those of their employers. Under his original proposals virtually everyone in paid employment would be required to contribute to a stakeholder insurance scheme which provided cover against unemployment and sickness, and also to take out a second private pension which would run alongside the existing National Insurance scheme. Both the new stakeholder insurance and the compulsory second pension would be so-called funded schemes. That is, the monies paid in on behalf of contributors would be invested and the proceeds used to fund their pensions and other benefits. The right to a pension and other benefits would thus be akin to property rights, since they would be paid out of an identifiable fund to which the recipient has contributed. All of this, Field argued, would make the benefits provided by the stakeholder scheme much less vulnerable to changes in public policy than were the existing National Insurance benefits.

This, however, did not resolve the central dilemma that if 'stakeholding' were to be an inclusive concept, then ways would have to be found of paying contributions on behalf of those unable to pay them for themselves. Field accepted that there can be no redistribution within the schemes from the better off to the poorer contributors, and so these contributions will have to be paid by government:

this redistribution – a word which radicals should not be afraid to use – needs to be above board, to be clearly of a targeted form, to be made and agreed by taxpayers as a whole, financed by the Exchequer, and on no account paid for by means of a surreptitious filching of funds from individual scheme-holders' accounts.

(Field 1997: 96)

In the final analysis, however, the fact that this redistribution would be 'above board' would not make it any easier to sell it to the voters at a time when, in Field's own memorable phrase, the 'age of the passive taxpayer is . . . moving peacefully to its close' (p. 64). Field acknowleged that taxpayers 'are likely to stump up a contribution for poorer stakeholders only if they approve of the behaviour of those for whom they are contributing' (pp. 24–5). It follows from this that the process of enlarging the ranks of stake-holders would have to be undertaken gradually – Field suggested starting with carers – and be accompanied by vigorous measures to combat benefit fraud. Even so, this still leaves much to be achieved by persuasion and argument, and it is at this point that the logic of self-interest finally runs out. If stakeholder welfare was to offer a means whereby the poor could be rescued from the tangle of means testing, then something other than self-interest would have to ensure that the taxpayers foot the bill.

This proved to be the Achilles' heel of Field's proposals. It will be seen in Chapter 7 that he was not able to persuade his Cabinet colleagues – and especially the Chancellor of the Exchequer, Gordon Brown – that it was possible to reduce the scope of the means test in the British welfare system. Nevertheless, Field's contribution remains a significant one, both for the development of New Labour thinking and for the broader themes of this book. Encouraged by Blair to 'think the unthinkable', Field did more than anyone on the centre left to challenge the quasi-Titmuss paradigm and to align New Labour with an older working-class tradition of self-improvement and mutual aid. It was, he argues, the friendly societies, building societies and other self-help organizations of the nineteenth century that struck a 'proper' balance between individual and structural factors in explaining social problems.

The individual was not demeaned as he or she is by so much of today's left wing ideology which puts all the emphasis on structural causes as the reasons for preventing personal advance. But neither was it naive in believing that the structural forces were without importance.

(Field 1997: 103)

Field's work remains the clearest guide to what a welfare system would look like if it sought to strike this 'proper balance' and to channel the self-interest of voters and claimants alike.

Conclusion: the limits of self-interest?

Charles Murray and Frank Field have different ideas about the ends of social policy, and about what constitutes the good society. For Murray the goal is a society that cherishes the liberty and freedom of choice of individuals, but then holds them accountable for the ways in which they exercise that choice. For Field, the goal is a society which is more inclusive, which recognizes the need for collective provision, but which also recognizes the responsibility of individuals to seek their own self-improvement through cooperative effort and mutual aid. What Murray and Field share is the conviction that whatever the ultimate objective of a welfare system may be, it will only attain that objective if its design and delivery recognizes that individuals are motivated primarily by self-interest. Welfare policies cannot attain their ends by coercion; nor can they rely on appeals to altruism. All they can do is create a framework that channels the individual pursuit of self-interest. In Murray's case the focus is almost entirely upon the impact of welfare benefits upon the poor; in Field's case the canvas is much broader. Neither, however, 'blame[s] the poor for responding rationally to the welfare framework which politicians impose upon them' (Field 1997: 16), and both assume that they will change their behaviour if that framework is reformed. The next chapter outlines a perspective that starts from a very different assumption.

Notes

1 This paragraph draws upon De Parle (1994) and private correspondence with Professor John Macnicol.
2 The significance of longitudinal data for an understanding of the nature and causes of poverty is explained in Chapters 5 and 7.
3 Murray's use of the term 'illegitimate' will be offensive to some readers, and is used here only in direct quotation from him. The term 'out-of-wedlock births' is used elsewhere in the book.

Further reading

The best introduction to Murray's ideas and the response to them in Britain is provided by Lister (1996). Less provocative but more interesting outlines of Murray's thinking can be found in the book *In Pursuit of Happiness and Good Government* (Murray 1988) and an article analysing longitudinal data on poverty in the USA (Murray 1987). There is now an enormous literature on the 'underclass debate', and excellent introductions to it are provided by Macnicol (1987, 1999) and Mann (1994). The best introduction to Field's thinking in opposition is provided by his essay and the accompanying critical commentaries in Deacon (1996). The subsequent development of his ideas is documented in two volumes of essays (Field 1997, 1998).

chapter

three

Welfare and paternalism

The differences between the perspective which is explored in this chapter and that of Charles Murray or Frank Field are simple and stark. 'The entire tradition of explaining poverty or dependency in terms of incentives or disincentives', writes Lawrence Mead (1992: 136), 'is bankrupt.' It is bankrupt, he argues, because the long-term poor do not respond to changes in the framework of financial incentives or sanctions in the way that Murray and Field presume. The reason why they do not respond is that they are not competent, functioning individuals who act rationally to further their interests. On the contrary, they are the 'dutiful but defeated' who will not take advantage of opportunities for advancement unless forced to do so.

The explanation of long-term poverty, then, lies not in the perverse incentives generated by welfare but in the character of the poor themselves and in a political culture that condones self-destructive behaviour. It follows that the solution is to be found not in the creation of new opportunities or financial inducements but in the exercise of authority. The role of welfare should be to compel the poor to behave in ways that are conducive to their long-term betterment, and thereby promote the common good. This can be achieved most readily by making their entitlement to benefits and services conditional upon their behaving in prescribed ways. The most obvious and important example of such conditionality is, of course, the imposition of work requirements upon applicants for unemployment benefits: **workfare**. Back in 1992, however, Mead argued that workfare was 'only the most developed instance of a trend', and wrote of a new paternalism in welfare: 'A tutelary regime is emerging in which dependents receive support of several kinds on condition of restrictions on their lives' (Mead 1992: 181). It is Mead himself who is by far the best known and most influential advocate of this paternalism, and it is with his arguments that this chapter is primarily concerned.

Lawrence Mead

There are striking parallels between the early careers of Charles Murray and Lawrence Mead. Both began in Washington in the 1970s. In Mead's case, he worked first as a policy analyst in the Department of Health, Education and Welfare, then as a researcher at the Urban Institute, and finally as Deputy Director of Research for the Republican Party in 1978–9. He subsequently became a career academic, and has taught political science at New York University for over twenty years. There is no doubt, however, that it was the experience of evaluating the federal programmes of the 1970s that shaped his thinking on welfare. As early as 1978, for example, he wrote an unpublished memorandum for the Republicans which argued that the central flaw in federal welfare policy was that it gave a higher priority to the transfer of 'income and in-kind benefits' to 'the needy' than it did to 'helping them function better as citizens'. As a result, the chief effect of the programmes was to produce a kind of 'economic reservation for the disadvantaged' and to shield them from the pressures which impinged on other Americans (Mead 1978: 6). The implication was that the poor would have to accept the same responsibilities and obligations as everyone else if they were to enjoy the same rights of citizenship. It was this argument which formed the cornerstone of Mead's first book, *Beyond Entitlement*.

Beyond Entitlement was first published in the USA towards the end of 1985, around a year after Murray's *Losing Ground*. Like Murray, Mead began by asking why 'federal programs since 1960 have coped so poorly with the various social problems that have come to afflict American society' (Mead 1986: 1). Mead's answer to this question, however, was very different to the one given in *Losing Ground*. Murray had focused upon the relative rewards of work and welfare, and had emphasized the rationality of those who chose dependency. For Mead the root of the problem was not the level of benefits but the terms and conditions on which they were paid.

> Part of the explanation, I propose, is that the federal programs that support the disadvantaged and unemployed have been permissive in character, not authoritative. That is, they have given benefits to their recipients but have set few requirements for how they ought to function in return.
>
> (Mead 1986: 1)

Simply withdrawing welfare as Murray had proposed would make matters worse, since 'many dependent people could not immediately cope on their own' (p. 4). The only solution was to continue to provide help, but to combine that help with clear requirements as to their conduct.

It will be seen in this chapter that one of the most striking features of Mead's writings is the consistency of his arguments and of the assumptions on which those arguments are based. For over twenty years he has put forward a series of propositions about both the justification for and the feasibility of paternalist interventions in the lives of poor people. He has defended and developed these ideas in debate with, among others, Charles Murray, William Julius Wilson and David Ellwood. In contrast to Murray, however, his basic position has remained unchanged. In consequence, it is more convenient to discuss these propositions in turn rather than to trace the development of Mead's thinking over time.

The obligations of citizenship

All of Mead's writings on welfare are grounded in one central assumption: that 'government's essential, if not only, purpose is to maintain public order' (Mead 1986: 5). By public order Mead does not mean just the containment of crime, but 'all of the social and economic conditions people depend on for satisfying lives, but which are government's responsibility rather than their own.' Even conservatives accept that these encompass the management of 'overall economic conditions' and the provision of basic public services. No government, however, can 'assure the conditions for order by itself': 'It depends upon the concurrence of people with government . . . Government is really a mechanism by which people force themselves to serve and obey *each other* in necessary ways' (pp. 5–6).

If people are to serve each other in this way, they have to be both self-disciplined and competent. Not only must they not harm others, but they have also to fulfil the expectations that others have of them as parents, as workers, as neighbours. Mead argued that this need for competence had been neglected in debates about citizenship.

> The capacities to learn, work, support one's family, and respect the rights of others amount to a set of *social* obligations alongside the political ones. A civic society might almost be defined as one in which people are competent in all these senses.
>
> (p. 6)

The goal of welfare, then, should be to contribute to a society in which all possess these capacities and in which all can enjoy equal citizenship.

> The great merit of equal citizenship as a social goal is that it is much more widely achievable than status. It is not competitive. It does not require that the disadvantaged 'succeed', something not everyone can do. It requires only that everyone discharge the common obligations.
>
> (p. 12)

The corollary, of course, is that those who do not function can never be equal with those who do. Indeed, it is this failure to meet the common obligations that delineates and defines the underclass. It is comprised, he wrote, 'of those Americans who combine relatively low income with functioning problems' (p. 22). More specifically, the underclass – which Mead sometimes terms the 'disavantaged' – consists of people who have been poor for more than two years, who are not elderly and do not have a disability which prevents them from working. All of Mead's arguments rest upon the assumption that the poverty of this specific group is caused by their behaviour, not by their circumstances. If they are socially excluded it is because they have excluded themselves. If they experience stigma it is because they have chosen to be dependent. 'For how can the dependent be equal, except in the most metaphysical sense, with those who support them?' (Mead 1986: 43).

It was seen in Chapter 2 that the perspectives of Titmuss and Charles Murray differed most sharply in respect of the issue of stigma. This is equally true of Titmuss and Mead. Whereas Titmuss had sought to avoid stigmatizing the poor by including them within universal benefits and services, Mead argued that this would be counter-productive: 'The case for universality assumes that changing the image of the programs will change the reputation of the poor. Unfortunately the reputation of the recipients seems rather to shape the image of the programs' (Mead 1997a: 209). There was, Mead argued, no alternative but to use compulsion to force the underclass to accept the obligations of citizenship. He acknowledged in *Beyond Entitlement* that some would not respond, and so would suffer still greater ostracism. That, however, was a price that had to be paid. Far from being a cause of stigma, paternalistic direction was the only way in which a majority of the underclass could escape from stigmatizing dependency. 'Society must give up at least some of its fear of "blaming the victim" if it is to help them more effectively. In part the choice it faces is whether to stigmatize the least cooperative of the disadvantaged in order to integrate the rest' (Mead 1986: 247).

The justification for paternalism, then, was that it could lead to the reintegration of the underclass. What made this reintegration feasible was the fact that it was what most of the underclass wanted all along. Mead has always claimed that the strength of paternalism is that it compels people to do what they know they should be doing anyway. The underclass, he argued in *Beyond Entitlement*, are 'distinctive not in their beliefs but in their inability to conform to them as closely as other people' (p. 22). The task of public policy, then, is not to condone the failure of the poor to conform to agreed social norms, but to 'close the gap between the norm and the welfare recipient's lifestyle' (Mead 1997b: 64). Traditional social policies cannot bridge this gap because they rest on what Mead calls the 'competence assumption' – the assumption that the individual is willing and able to advance his or her own economic interests (Mead 1992: 19).

It is Mead's rejection of this assumption that distances him from the other writers discussed in this book. In repudiation of Murray he insists that 'the disincentives of welfare' are 'insufficient to explain the extent of nonwork and female-headed households' among the poor (p. 118). Furthermore, it is an 'abuse of language' to describe such behaviour as rational, since rationality must involve foresight (p. 136). At the same time he rejects the argument put forward by Myron Magnet in *The Dream and the Nightmare* (1993) that the main cause of poverty lies in the insidious impact upon the poor of the counter-culture of the 1960s. This enables Mead to claim that his own position is a 'moderate one': 'It rejects the position that nonwork is sensible behaviour for the poor, and also the view that the poor are fundamentally flawed or opposed to work. I see them rather as dutiful but defeated' (Mead 1992: 133). It is because the long-term poor are so 'defeated' that they will not respond to the financial incentives. Attempts to 'make work pay', claims Mead, are popular with liberals because they assume that all of the poor 'respond to the same suasions as the middle class'. The reality, however, is that 'the people who respond to incentives are mainly those who are already functional, already within the economy'. Incentives could not 'pull many people across the line from nonwork to work' (p. 162). This could be achieved only through the strict enforcement of work requirements. 'The main problem', Mead says, 'lies not with the poor themselves but with political authorities who refuse to govern them firmly' (Mead 1986: 248).

It follows from this that the proper implementation of paternalism will require a transformation in the role of government. The essence of paternalism is, of course, the exercise of authority. Not only is an individual's entitlement to welfare subject to conditions as to his or her behaviour, but the fulfilment of those conditions is enforced through direction and surveillance. Those who are dependent upon welfare are not to be offered new opportunities, not to be given new incentives. They are to be told how to conduct themselves in at least some aspects of their lives. Moreover, paternalism holds that this authority is being exercised for their own good as well as that of the wider society. There is, it believes, a harmony of interests insofar as enforcing society's interest in good behaviour also serves the long-term interests of the dependent. All of this challenges head on the central tenet of Western liberal philosophy, expressed most famously in John Stuart Mill's 'harm principle':

> The only purpose for which power can rightfully be exercised over any member of a civilised community, against his will, is to prevent harm to others. His own good, either physical or moral, is not sufficient warrant. He cannot rightfully be compelled to do or forbear because, in the opinion of others, to do so would be wise, or even right.
>
> (Mill, quoted in Selznick 1998a: 10)

As another advocate of paternalism, Mark Kleiman, has noted, Mill's case for 'perfect liberty' applied to 'self-regarding actions'. It assumed that it was 'the nature of human beings to make good choices for themselves', and that 'there is no gain to be had in regulating their actions except where those actions affect others' (Kleiman 1997: 187). Mead's argument is that this assumption is false in respect of the long-term poor, and that the Western liberal tradition now has nothing to say about the 'painful issues of dependency'. In its place 'a new tradition, even a new political theory must be created' (Mead 1992: 211).

Alongside this new political theory must come a 'reinvention of welfare administration'. Mead argues that the essentially reactive approach of traditional public administration is ill-equipped to deal with the passivity of the underclass. The most successful workfare programmes are those which have high expectations of their clients and which communicate those expectations through intensive case management. Mead quotes the manager of one such scheme in Riverside, California, by way of illustration. 'It's really simple: you've got to be all over every client like flypaper! Everyday' (Mead 1997b: 62). It is this combination of 'help and hassle' which Mead sees as the defining characteristic of the authoritative approach to welfare. At the same time he concedes that it places great demands upon bureaucracies that 'in many localities' have 'endured popular scorn and drawn few talented employees for decades' (p. 72). It is for this reason that as late as 1997 Mead was predicting that 'paternalistic welfare reform' would not 'come quickly' and would be limited to states such as Wisconsin where the necessary political and institutional framework was in place (p. 74).

Lawrence Mead, then, has presented a range of arguments in support of paternalism. Indeed, the debate has resembled a series of 'Punch and Judy' shows, in which he has used the alleged demise of the competence assumption as a conceptual stick with which to batter a range of adversaries from the libertarian right to the egalitarian left. Thus far, however, this chapter has focused upon Mead's own arguments. It has said nothing about the attacks that have been made upon his position.

Mead and his critics

By far the most important criticism that has been made of paternalism is that it lacks any empirical foundation. However logical Mead's reasoning, however persuasive his prose, the fact remains that his argument for workfare rests upon two central assumptions. The first of these is that the poor do not work because they lack the necessary competencies and character. The second is that this failure to work is the central cause of long-term poverty and dependency.

To liberals, the first assumption is simply false. Mead himself acknowledges that workfare 'depends critically on jobs being available' (Mead 1988a: 42). In reality, they argue, there is no convincing evidence that there are anything like enough jobs to get everyone off welfare. Moreover, many of those that do exist do not pay enough to lift a family out of poverty. How, they ask, can Mead be so dogmatic about the functioning problems of the poor when many could not get a job however hard they tried?

At the same time, many conservatives are highly sceptical about the first assumption. What if non-work is not a cause of dependency but a symptom of deeper pathologies which arise from the collapse of the two-parent family? How, they ask, does it benefit a child in a female-headed household to compel his or her mother to take a paid job? The problem with such households, they argue, is not the absence of a job but the absence of a male partner.

The 'jobs' debate

The availability of at least low-paid work was asserted rather than argued in *Beyond Entitlement*. The problem, Mead wrote, was that many of those on welfare were not 'job seeking' but 'job shopping'. By this he meant that they were not prepared to take any job that was on offer but only one that they found attractive, and then only if someone else had already resolved the problem of child care (Mead 1986: 80). The book, however, contained little evidence that the poor did behave in this way, save for the observation that some ten million illegal aliens had 'had little trouble in finding employment' (p. 35).

The most serious challenge to Mead's assumptions about work came from the economist David Ellwood – who is the subject of Chapter 5 – and the sociologist William Julius Wilson. Like Mead, Wilson believes that the behaviour of the poor themselves is an important part of any explanation of the rise of inner-city poverty. Indeed, it was seen in Chapter 1 that he has long been critical of the reluctance of many liberals to discuss openly the growth of social pathologies in the ghetto. The central difference between them is that whereas Mead sees the attitudes and behaviours of the 'under-class' as a cause of non-work, Wilson sees them as a consequence of it. The defeatism described by Mead is, according to Wilson, an adaptation to circumstances imposed upon the ghetto by external forces. In *The Truly Disadvantaged*, published in 1987, Wilson argued that the 'key theoretical concept' was not 'the culture of poverty' but 'social isolation'. This was not because 'cultural traits' were unimportant in understanding behaviour but because those traits were themselves 'a response to social structural constraints and opportunities' (Wilson 1987: 61). Thus 'the inner-city social dislocations' which so concerned Murray and Mead 'should be analyzed not as cultural aberrations but as symptoms of racial-class inequalities' (p. 159).

In a later book, *When Work Disappears* (1997), Wilson set out in detail the socio-economic forces which have produced these 'racial-class inequalities': the collapse of manufacturing industry in the inner city, the flight of the black middle class to the suburbs and the mismatch between the skills and experience of ghetto residents and those demanded by the employers who remain. Above all he emphasized the way in which these forces reinforced each other to transform the institutional ghetto – 'whose structure and activities parallel those of the larger society' – into the jobless ghetto – 'which features a severe lack of basic opportunities and resources, and inadequate social controls (Wilson 1997: 23).

In all his writings Wilson stresses the complexity of the interaction between cultural and material factors. It may be rational, for example, for lone mothers to remain on welfare rather than to accept a low-paid job. Nevertheless, it is still much easier to take that decision in the ghetto than it is in areas where many neighbours are working and expect them to do the same: 'their decisions are made easier in two ways: the greater frequency with which similar decisions are made by other mothers in the neighborhood and the more tolerant neighborhood attitude towards welfare receipt' (p. 87). Similarly, the severity of the decline in marriage rates cannot be explained in purely cultural or economic terms, but only by a combination of the two. High rates of unemployment make it harder for men to support families, and thus undermine the traditional two-parent family. The consequent growth in female-headed households weakens communal norms against out-of-wedlock births, and this further increases the influence of financial considerations upon decisions to marry (Wilson 1997: 97).

Wilson is not, of course, the only person to stress the complexity of the influences upon behaviour in the ghetto. What is important here is the way in which he cited that complexity to dismiss the idea that 'one can address the problems of the ghetto underclass by simply emphasising the social obligations of citizenship'. Despite Mead's 'eloquent arguments', he concluded, 'the empirical support for his thesis is incredibly weak' (Wilson 1987: 161).

Mead responded to these criticisms in three ways. First, he shifted his position on some points. He accepted that the mismatch between the skills of inner-city residents and the needs of local employers may explain some of the unemployment in cities such as Chicago, which was the location for much of the research reported in *The Truly Disadvantaged* and *When Work Disappears*. He also acknowledged that it might be necessary to raise the quality of available jobs 'through raising the minimum wage or providing universal health insurance, before we can mandate them'. 'Job enrichment measures may have to join with enforcement in a new "social contract" before the inner-city work problem can be solved' (Mead 1987: 13). What is particularly interesting about this statement is that it is the closest Mead has come to accepting the idea that governments and welfare claimants have mutual or reciprocal obligations towards each other. It will be seen in the following chapters that different formulations of this idea have underpinned the welfare reform proposals of both David Ellwood and many communitarians. In Mead's case, however, it was immediately qualified by the seemingly contradictory assertion that this should happen 'only after nonworkers accept the jobs that exist'. The core principle remained that only 'function-ing citizens' should be able 'to claim new economic rights'.

These concessions aside, Mead's general response to Wilson was to defend and develop his original arguments. He insisted that the structural changes outlined by Wilson could not explain more than one-third of the low work levels among the long-term poor. The problem was not that they could not find a job, but that they were unable or unwilling to keep it. The essential difference between himself and Wilson was that Wilson believed that it was reasonable for the poor to leave or refuse jobs that they found unattractive. 'Job quality, not quantity, is the real issue in work enforcement. Many of those, including Wilson, who oppose workfare on the grounds that jobs are unavailable really seem to mean that they are unacceptable' (Mead 1987: 13).

This was the starting point for Mead's third and most significant response to Wilson. The availability of jobs, he argued, was not a technical issue, resolvable by data, but a question of standards. It was possible, for example, to regard as unemployed anyone who expressed a wish to work, or to count only those who made continual and extensive efforts to find work. Con-versely, a job may be any employment which is within the law, or only that which is offered on particular terms and conditions. 'These assumptions', he said, are 'terribly sensitive, and neither conservatives nor liberals have wanted to be explicit about them' (Mead 1988a: 42). Nevertheless, they determined the view that was taken of the labour market.

> If one defines acceptable jobs broadly but employability narrowly, as conservatives do, jobs will seem widely available. Equally if one sets more demanding standards for jobs but lower ones for workers as lib-erals do, jobs will seem lacking.
>
> (p. 52)

This means, of course, that it only makes sense to impose work requirements on a conservative view of the labour market. The problems which liberals see as barriers to employment – such as a lack of training or a shortage of child care – are regarded by conservatives as 'the ordinary logistics of work-ing, which the poor, like other people, can handle by themselves' (Mead 1991: 14). For all the 'arcane statistics' which are so often cited, the jobs debate is really about the capacities of the poor, and what can be demanded of them.

> The real issue is whether the worker should be held responsible for meeting the needs of the economy or vice versa. Whereas conservatives project the demands of the economy onto the poor, liberals project the needs of the poor onto the economy. Who should adapt to whom?
>
> (Mead 1988a: 54)

The debate between Mead and Wilson is a fascinating exploration of the differences between an individualist and a structural account of poverty and unemployment. The exchanges, however, could never be conclusive. Neither Mead nor Wilson would ever convince the other because their broader objectives were totally different. It was seen in Chapter 1 that Wilson is an egalitarian. He seeks to make the labour market more attractive to the poor as one step towards a more inclusive society. For his part, Mead takes both the labour market and the broader distribution of resources as given, and believes that the poor should take what jobs they can find – as everyone else has to.

It is scarcely necessary to add that Mead and Wilson would use very different criteria to assess the success or failure of workfare. For Mead it is the actual experience of workfare that provides the only conclusive test of whether or not jobs are available. If people do indeed move from welfare to work then that is a vindication of his position. It would not matter if many of the jobs were low-paid because they would still represent the first rung on a ladder. Having crossed the line from dependency to work, the former claimant would in time acquire the work record and experience she needed for a better job. For Wilson, on the other hand, it would not be the size of the welfare caseload that mattered, but the numbers in poverty. It would be punitive to force large numbers of women to take menial jobs that left them and their children in poverty, and he would continue to stress the need to create more jobs and to make those jobs pay. This debate is considered further in Chapter 6. The next step here is to consider the other main challenge to Mead's position – that it ignores the importance of family structure.

Non-work and the family

It was seen in Chapter 2 that from the early 1990s Charles Murray had begun to argue that the key to tackling the underclass was not to impose work requirements upon female-headed households but to deter the formation of such families in the first place. Even if welfare reform did succeed 'in moving large numbers of women off the welfare rolls' it would still have achieved 'nothing' unless it also reduced the 'illegitimacy ratio' (Murray 1998: 61). A further criticism made by both conservative and liberal opponents of workfare was that it would be against the interests of children to compel their mothers to work. In the 1980s and early 1990s this argument was used by liberals to defend AFDC. As Jencks and Edin (1990: 46) noted at the time: 'Today the only way to justify paying women to stay at home and care for their children is to claim that this will be good for the children, not the mothers.' Similarly, the conservative James Q. Wilson argued that child protection was the most important goal: 'Surely we wish to protect the next generation from neglect more than we wish mothers to work. Requiring work may reduce welfare rolls but we are not certain that it improves children' (Wilson 1997: 342).

Mead's response to the first of these criticisms is a pragmatic one. In *Beyond Entitlement* he had traced the 'functioning problems' of the 'underclass' to 'an unstable family life marked by absent fathers, erratic parenting, and low self esteem and aspiration' (Mead 1986: 22). If anything he repeated this argument with growing rather than diminishing force in later years. In 1991, for example, he claimed that the 'inequalities that stem from the workplace are now trivial in comparison to those stemming from family structure . . . What matters for success is less whether your father was rich or poor than whether you knew your father at all' (Mead 1991: 10). Mead goes on, however, to argue that effective public policy requires more than the identification of a problem. It helps to have some idea of a solution. In the case of 'illegitimacy' no such solution is in sight. Government 'knows something about how to enforce work, but almost nothing about how to confine childbearing to marriage' (Mead 1997b: 69).

Mead's response to the second criticism is equally pragmatic. It may be true that the 'main task of social policy' is now to 'restore the authority of parents and other mentors who shape citizens', but there is 'no easy way' for governments to achieve this. The best they can do is to 'require that poor parents work, because employment failures are the greatest cause of family failures'. If the parents do not function, 'no programme to help the children can achieve much' (Mead 1997d: 15).

The new paternalism

It has to be said that the question as to whether or not it is beneficial for young children if their mothers are required to take a paid job is not one that looms large in current policy debates in the USA. It will be seen in Chapter 6 that it is now taken as read that such mothers should be in paid employment. A more immediate issue in the USA is how far paternalism offers a remedy for the other ways in which 'underclass families' are allegedly failing to function. If it is feasible to compel welfare mothers to work, then why not also require them to attend high school or to keep off drugs? In addition they can be required to ensure that their children attend school regularly, or that their children receive the immunization injections they needed.

The rationale for this new paternalism is underpinned by some very old political ideas. This is the argument, derived from Aristotle, that the development of moral character requires self-discipline and the acquisition of good habits. People become virtuous by the practice of virtue. They acquire self-control by the exercise of self-control. It is precisely this process that can be undermined by unconditional or indiscriminate welfare, but which can be reinforced by the supervision and direction provided by paternalistic welfare.

Back in 1985, James Q. Wilson had drawn upon the same ideas to argue that the problem of welfare dependency required a return to the 'traditional view' that the goal of politics was to 'improve the character' of the people. The Founders of the American Republic had acted on a very different understanding, that of 'taking human nature pretty much as it was'. They had framed a constitution that protected the freedom of the individual from government through a careful balance of the powers of the legislature, the executive and the judiciary. They had assumed that government would be indifferent towards the processes of character formation, but that indifference could not be sustained if public policy was to respond effectively to such issues as family breakdown, criminality and dependency.

> The essential first step is to acknowledge that at root, in almost every area of important public concern, we are seeking to induce persons to act virtuously . . . By virtue I mean habits of moderate action; more specifically, acting with due restraint on one's impulses, due regard for the rights of others, and reasonable concern for distant consequences.
>
> (Wilson 1985: 15)

Writing 12 years later, he argued that paternalism had to be 'enlarged and extended' in order to deal with those 'who have by their behaviour indicated that they do not display the minimal level of self control expected of decent citizens'. These included 'deadbeat dads, unmarried teenage mothers, and single mothers claiming welfare benefits' (Wilson 1997: 341).

Not all the new paternalist programmes are as punitive as Wilson's rhetoric may suggest. Among the most innovative are the so-called 'fragile families' projects that seek to rebuild relationships between 'absent fathers' and the mothers of their children. These are paternalist insofar as the fathers are compelled to participate and are subject to close personal supervision. At the same time they are given considerable help to find work so that they can meet their child support obligations (Mincy and Pouncy 1997). Other examples include projects for homeless men that require hostel residents to sign up to an 'independent living plan' and to receive treatment for addiction and/or mental health problems (Main 1997) and projects which require teenage mothers on welfare to participate in a range of educational, health and training programmes (Maynard 1997). Indeed, one reason why a more authoritative approach has become so attractive to some politicians in the United States is that it seems to offer something to both parties. As Paul Starobin observed in 1998, it appealed to Democrats who viewed their association with traditional welfare as an electoral handicap, and to Republicans who were seeking 'an activist ideology that keeps faith with conservative principles'. The new paternalists – or 'Daddy Staters' as he called them – thus occupied 'the most-desired ground in American politics: the middle' (Starobin 1998: 1).

Conclusion: the limits of paternalism?

In 1991 Robert Walker reviewed the development of welfare to work programmes in the USA and concluded that the 'American evidence is clear, workfare works best as an ideology' (Walker 1991: 55). The extent to which this judgement still stands is considered in Chapter 6. There is no question, however, that it is a reasonable assessment of the broader forms of the new paternalism. Indeed, the advocates of paternalism have made relatively muted claims of what can be achieved beyond the enforcement of work requirements. Rebecca Maynard (1997: 101), for example, comments that after 'more than a decade of research, observers have found no magic formula for the prevention of teenage pregnancies'. Similarly, Mincy and Pouncy (1997: 131) report that the results of the 'fragile family' experiments are 'uncertain but encouraging'.

Those who advocate paternalism recognize two central difficulties. The first, as noted above, is the capacity of welfare bureaucracies, and especially the lack of staff with the requisite skills and experience. The second, more significant, difficulty concerns the long-term effects of paternalistic direction. By definition paternalism means treating the dependent poor like children, not in itself the most obvious way of promoting self-reliance and self-discipline. Even if the individualistic assumptions that underpin paternalism are accepted, the question remains as to what happens when the direction ceases. In Mark Kleiman's words, it is still necessary to ask 'whether it tends to ameliorate or exacerbate the deficits in self-command that gave rise to the need for such intervention in the first place' (Kleiman 1997: 191).

Mead himself recognizes that if paternalism is to be truly effective then it will have to lead to changes in the culture of low-income communities. There will have to be a new consensus that fosters and inculcates the values of responsibility and self-reliance. Government paternalism, he concedes, was not needed in the past on anything like the scale he now advocates precisely because such values were upheld by informal networks and private forms of social control.

> It is possible that public paternalism might help regenerate those informal controls, partly by involving community organizations in directive programs and partly by legitimizing the idea – in and outside government – that social norms can and should be enforced.
> (Mead 1997c: 28)

It is at this point that the boundary between paternalism and some forms of communitarianism becomes somewhat blurred. The overlap between these two perspectives is discussed further in the next chapter.

Further reading

A good introduction to the British debate about workfare is provided by Mead's essay and the accompanying critical commentaries in Deacon (1997). The best examples of Mead's writings are two articles in *Public Interest* (1988a, 1991), and the debate with William Julius Wilson in *Focus* (1987). The influence of the authoritarian perspective upon European welfare regimes is discussed in Lodemal and Trickey (2001), and the adoption of compulsion in Britain is chronicled in King and Wickam-Jones (1999). The extent to which workfare should be extended to lone mothers in Britain is debated by Duncan and Edwards (1997, 1999), Phillips (1997a, b) and Lister (1999). The central source for the broader application of paternalism in the USA is the volume of essays edited by Mead (1997), and the debate between Mead and Murray is discussed further in Deacon (2001).

chapter

four

Welfare and obligation

The perspective that is discussed in this chapter starts from the premise that people sometimes act out of a sense of commitment. They are not always motivated by either self-interest or altruism. Nor do they necessarily have to be compelled to behave in ways that serve the common good. Instead they may act in a particular way because they feel that they have to do so in order to fulfil an obligation. That obligation may be to their immediate family, to communities of place or faith or to the wider society. It may be rooted in blood ties, emotional commitments, religious or philosophical convictions or simply in an acceptance of the need to reciprocate benefits or services received. What matters is that at least some of the time they are motivated by a sense of duty rather than a desire for betterment or a fear of punishment.

The focus of this chapter is upon those who argue that the central objective of welfare should be to foster and enhance just this sense of duty and of commitment. From this perspective welfare should look primarily to persuasion rather than to compulsion, to encouragement and to moral argument rather than to financial inducements or penalties. Such arguments are associated most closely with communitarianism. As Amitai Etzioni (1998: xii) notes, a prominent theme of recent communitarian writing is that 'much of social conduct is, and that more ought to be, sustained and guided by an informal web of social bonds and moral voices of the community.' These new or so-called 'responsive' communitarians have sought to demonstrate that it is both desirable and possible to 'rely first and foremost on attempts to persuade, rather than coerce, people when seeking to promote pro-social behaviour' (*ibid.*: xiii).

These claims are examined in this chapter. It begins by outlining some of the central tenets of communitarian thinking, before discussing the work of the best known communitarian writer, Amitai Etzioni. The third and fourth sections provide a brief outline of two recent discussions of communitarian ideas, by Rabbi Jonathan Sacks in Britain and Phillip Selznick in the United States. The fifth and final section attempts to identify the major themes of a communitarian approach to welfare.

This chapter, then, differs from the previous three chapters in that it does not focus as specifically upon the work of one or two individuals. This change of approach is necessary because the perspective outlined here differs from those discussed earlier in three important respects. First, the communitarian literature is much broader in scope. Communitarians have much to say about the role of welfare but it is not their primary concern, as it is for Titmuss, Murray or Mead. Second, the communitarian literature is a very diverse one. Not all of those whose work is discussed here would accept the label, while those who do differ sharply in their attitudes towards the family, equality or the proper role of government. It is for this reason that communitarianism has been derided as a 'flexi-philosophy' by its critics (Milne 1994: 5). Third, the breadth and diversity of communitarian writing means that the distinctions between it and the other perspectives are not always as clear-cut as those between Titmuss and Murray, or even those between Murray and Mead.

Nevertheless, it must be emphasized again that to highlight the commonalities between perspectives is not to suggest that they are the same. The communitarian perspective on welfare is a distinctive one. It is also one which has had a significant influence upon the approach to welfare reform in both Britain and the United States.

'Responsive' communitarianism

Modern communitarianism emerged in the 1980s as a response to what its advocates saw as the excessive **individualism** of contemporary Western societies. Its central claim is that this excessive individualism has produced a profound and damaging imbalance. Far too much attention is paid to the rights of individuals, the enjoyment of which safeguards their freedom and enhances their personal autonomy. Far too little attention is paid to the social responsibilities of those individuals, the acceptance of which maintains social order and enhances the communities in which they live. Nowhere is this imbalance more stark or more fiercely defended than it is in the United States, and much communitarian theory has been forged in a bitter debate with libertarians on both the left and right of American politics.

This context is important because communitarians are quick to point out that other societies are characterized by an excess of conformism. Were they in South East Asia, they claim, they would be the first to argue for greater personal freedom. Indeed, it is on this basis that they distinguish themselves from older forms of communitarianism that often neglected the danger that communities could easily become authoritarian and exclusive.

At the core of this modern or 'responsive' communitarianism, however, are three much older beliefs that are shared by the writers discussed in this chapter and are crucial to an understanding of their perspective on welfare. The first is the belief that liberty is not licence, and that the former requires a measure of self-restraint on the part of individuals. The second is the belief in the existence of a common good, which can be identified and pursued through collective deliberation and action. The third is the belief that individuals possess a moral sense, which disposes them to make moral judgements and to heed the moral judgements of others.

Liberty as autonomy

Communitarians start from the premise that freedom should never be confused with self-indulgence or what Spragens calls 'acquiescence to inclination'. Rather, it should be understood as 'autonomy – the independence of action proper to a rational being' (Spragens 1998: 23). To exercise such autonomy, however, the individual must possess qualities of self-restraint and self-governance. Moreover, these qualities are not innate, nor can they be acquired in isolation. Instead they are fostered and shaped by interaction with others, and especially by the expectations of family, friends and local communities. It is these pressures and expectations that constitute the cultural foundations of a free society. As Phillip Selznick (1998a: 10) puts it, 'participation in a viable culture is an indispensable source of personal stability and social discipline.'

Communitarians go on to claim that this 'culture' is threatened by the dominance of libertarianism, or 'radical individualism'. In the communitarian account, the defining characteristic of libertarianism is the overwhelming importance that it places upon personal freedom. In particular, communitarians argue, libertarianism fails to distinguish between the domain of politics and public affairs and the domain of private morality. This leads libertarians to extend the same tolerance and acceptance of diversity to personal behaviour as they do to religious beliefs and political allegiances. As Spragens (1998: 28) puts it,

> Libertarians tend to assume that the behavioural norms appropriate for a liberal society are the same as the political norms appropriate for liberal governments . . . The assumption is that the ideal of political toleration and government neutrality entails a thorough social permissiveness and moral relativism.

For communitarians this is a fatal error which leads inexorably to the demoralization of society. It has this effect because the personal virtues and qualities that underpin civil society are fostered and transmitted across the generations in families and local communities of faith and calling. These families and communities are not liberal institutions. They cannot allow people to exercise freedom of choice and still remain members. In Jonathan Sacks's words, they depend upon concepts like tradition, authority, loyalty and duty. 'Their very existence depends on our ability to suspend the choosing "I" in favour of the "We" of belonging and obligation' (Sacks 1997: 145). There are, then, severe limits to the extent to which these institutions can tolerate diversity among their members. At the same time they are the place 'where we learn habits essential to a free society', and the cultural contradiction of individualism is that it corrodes the very institutions upon which liberty depends.

The common good

Communitarians believe that it is possible to speak of a common good or public interest over and above the private interests and personal goals of individuals. Phillip Selznick, for example, argues that democracy is essentially 'a way of exercising collective will', a means of arriving at a collectively established conception of what will make the community better or worse off (Selznick 1998a: 11). Individuals cannot be left to decide for themselves what are and are not appropriate standards of behaviour. In the words of the Responsive Communitarian Platform (1998: xxxvi),

Reflecting the diverse moral voices of their citizens, responsive communities define what is expected of people, they educate their members to accept these values, and they praise them when they do and frown upon them when they do not.

Communitarianism, then, emphasizes both the obligations of individuals and the role of the community in ensuring that those obligations are met. It will be apparent that communitarians share much of the judgementalism of conservatives such as Murray or Mead. Indeed, what is most distinctive about communitarianism is its belief in the power of informal social networks and of moral argument to bring about significant and lasting changes in personal behaviour.

For this to happen two conditions have to be met. First, communities have to agree upon the criteria with which they will decide what is and what is not reasonable behaviour. Second, a high proportion of those who are 'frowned upon' have to accept the moral claims made upon them by the community and change their behaviour without being compelled to do so. Neither of these things can happen unless people possess what James Q. Wilson calls a 'moral sense'.

The moral senses

The debate about the existence of a moral sense raises issues of the most fundamental kind. What is universal about human nature? Are there moral sentiments which are common to peoples across the centuries and irrespective of race, gender, culture or the socio-economic development of the societies in which they live? Is human behaviour socially learned? Or is it innate, the product of natural selection over millennia?

These are difficult questions and their relevance to the debate about welfare reform is not immediately obvious. They are, however, central to the perspective that is discussed in this chapter. For if there is nothing universal about human nature, and if what is regarded as virtuous behaviour depends upon circumstances, then people are free to choose the values they live by and there is no basis for the kind of moral judgements that communitarians wish to make.

A powerful and highly influential argument for the existence of a moral sense has been put forward by James Q. Wilson in his book *The Moral Sense* (1993). James Q. Wilson is one of America's leading conservative intellectuals. It was seen in Chapters 2 and 3 that he was one of the first to criticize Murray's neglect of 'character', and that he has been an important influence upon the development of paternalism. He is perhaps best known, however, for his writings on criminality and his advocacy of a policy of 'zero tolerance' of minor crimes and incivilities.

Wilson says that his purpose in writing *The Moral Sense* was to 'help people to recover the confidence with which they once spoke about virtue and morality' and to 're-establish the possibility and the reasonableness of speaking frankly and convincingly about moral choices' (Wilson 1993: vii). Wilson's starting point is that people retain an intuition about what is right and wrong, and routinely make judgements about the behaviour and character of others in everyday conversations. Such judgements, however, are often excluded from public debates about the family, education or welfare. In part this is because most people have a commendable reluctance to appear intolerant or authoritarian, and do not wish to impose their beliefs and convictions upon others. For Wilson, however, it also reflects the influence of intellectuals who effectively deny the possibility of moral choices. The 'spirit of the age' is to accept diversity and to grant equal recognition and respect to different patterns of social organization and of personal behaviour. The result is a policy debate which talks about lifestyles rather than character and about values rather than virtues. 'Our reluctance to speak of morality and our suspicion, nurtured by our best minds, that we cannot "prove" our moral principles has amputated our public discourse at the knees' (Wilson 1993: xi).

The first step in restoring that public discourse is to acknowledge that people possess 'an intuitive or directly felt belief about how one ought to act when one is free to act voluntarily' (p. xii). It is this 'natural moral sense' that 'shapes human behaviour and the judgements people make of the behaviour of others' (p. 2). Wilson argues that what is universal in human nature is not behaviour but the sentiments that give rise to moral feelings and predispose men and women to behave in particular ways. Wilson gives four examples of these sentiments, which have been selected over 'eons of evolutionary history': sympathy, duty, self-control and fairness. Behaviour is thus the product of the interaction of these sentiments and 'the realities of economic circumstances, social structures, and family systems'. It follows that the immense variety of conditions will produce 'an equally great variety' of behaviours and of rules and customs by which those behaviours are regulated (p. 225). Most obviously, the expression of individual sentiments is shaped by culture. There is, for example, a common disposition to value fairness, but it is culture which determines 'who is equal to whom': 'Whether equal effort by kings and commoners, blacks and whites, or men and women should be thought of as constituting equal claims for reward is very much a matter of custom' (p. 72). A further complication is the fact that the individual moral sentiments can conflict with one another. The actions prompted by a disposition to be sympathetic, for example, may be the opposite of those prompted by a sense of duty. Moreover, the moral sense as a whole is counter-balanced by other aspects of human nature. 'Our selfish desires and moral capacities are at war with one another', writes Wilson, 'and often the former triumphs over the latter' (p. 11).

What links all of this to welfare is the notion of character. For Wilson a person of good character is someone who is able to strike a delicate balance between the individual moral sentiments, and between them and self-interest. This balance, however, is not struck after careful deliberation or reasoned argument. It is acquired by habit. It is through their repeated expression that moral sentiments become moral habits and moral habits come to constitute good character. The forum within which this occurs is the family, and welfare can foster this process or it can inhibit it.

Much of this is common ground between Wilson and the communitarian liberals discussed earlier in this section. They both believe that the acquisition of moral habits is essential if individuals are to exercise the self-restraint which proper autonomy requires. More than anything else, however, it is the idea of commitment which links Wilson and the communitarians, and which both seek to place at the heart of the welfare debate. For Wilson what is most important about moral sentiments is the fact that 'they have in common – in their origin and their maintenance – the notion of commitment' (Wilson 1993: 230). In contrast, the ideologies and intellectual tendencies which dominate contemporary debates have sought to replace the idea of commitment with the idea of choice. It is, Wilson argues, 'the fatally flawed assumption of many Enlightenment thinkers' that 'autonomous individuals can freely choose, or will, their moral life.'

> Believing that individuals are everything, rights are trumps, and morality is relative to time and place, such thinkers have been led to design

laws, practices, and institutions that leave nothing between the state and the individual save choices, contracts and entitlements.

(p. 250)

Communitarianism seeks to fill this breach by balancing choice with commitment, contracts with covenants and entitlements with obligations. Such a transformation is possible only if the moral sentiments identified by Wilson are first acknowledged and then nurtured within a regenerated moral environment. The most ambitious formulation of this strategy, and of welfare's place within it, has been provided by Amitai Etzioni.

Amitai Etzioni

Amitai Etzioni is a sociologist. He differs from some of the writers discussed in the earlier chapters in that he was already a prominent figure in the academic and policy-making communities in the United States before writing the books considered here. His reputation rested in part upon academic studies of organizations, the impact of technology and the nature of civil society; and in part upon his role as a White House Special Advisor to President Jimmy Carter in the early 1980s.

By Etzioni's own account, the catalyst for the ideas discussed below was a survey finding that a majority of young Americans believed that they had a right to be tried by a jury, but would not serve on a jury themselves. This position was clearly untenable, since the jury system cannot survive if people will not serve. It also 'violates a profound moral precept: that it is unfair to take and not to give, to draw on the commonwealth but to refuse to contribute' (Etzioni 1998: xvi). Etzioni became convinced that this attitude towards juries was indicative of a wider 'malaise'. People were demanding more from the government but were expecting to pay less in taxes, and they were claiming more rights but recognizing fewer obligations to the community. Any effective response to this malaise would have to begin by developing a 'third social philosophy' which rejected both libertarianism and authoritarian conservatism. Along with William Galston, Etzioni began inviting potential supporters to contribute to what eventually became the Responsive Communitarian Platform, issued in November 1991. This statement of communitarian principles was followed in 1993 by Etzioni's *The Spirit of Community* (British edition 1995).

As much a manifesto as a book, *The Spirit of Community* expressed many of the themes discussed in the previous section in direct, popular language. Etzioni's basic message was that the 'established but unfair' society of the 1950s had been swept away in the 1960s, but that nothing had filled 'the empty spaces that were left'. The traditional values had been discriminatory and authoritarian but their demise had not been followed by a 'solid affirmation of new values'. The result was confusion. 'We often cannot tell right from wrong – or cannot back up what we do believe in' (Etzioni 1995: 24). Similarly, the 1980s had elevated the 'unbridled pursuit of self-interest and greed to the level of social virtue'. An economy may thrive if 'people watched out only for themselves' but no society could function well given such 'self-centred, me-istic orientations'. The task was thus to 'shore up the moral foundations of society' and 'restore civic virtues' (p. 24).

The Spirit of Community was a best-seller in the United States. It was also highly contentious. Lauded as 'wonderful' by President Bill Clinton, it was roundly condemned as authoritarian and anti-feminist, and for extolling the virtues of small town conservatism. Etzioni has subsequently set out his version of the communitarian agenda more formally and at greater length in *The New Golden Rule* (1997).

The 'new golden rule'

The New Golden Rule is not a modest book. Nor does is lack ambition. Etzioni begins with the claim that 'communitarian thinking leapfrogs the old debate between left-wing and right-wing thinking and suggests a third social philosophy.' He also sets out to redraw 'the intellectual–political map'. Whereas the old map was centred on 'the role of government versus that of the private sector', the new map is centred on the 'relationship between the individual and the community, and between freedom and order' (Etzioni 1997: 7). 'The communitarian quest' is thus to find and maintain a balance between 'universal individual rights and the common good' and 'between self and community' (p. xviii).

The communitarian ideal is what Etzioni calls a normative moral order. This is a society in which order is maintained by appeals to common values and by moral argument, rather than by economic incentives or the exercise of authority. How far such a society is possible depends upon the degree of tension that exists between that which people would like to do – their preferences – and that which they are required to do – their commitments or their duties. The more people accept their duties as reasonable, the more the social order can be based upon 'normative means'.

> For a social order to be able to rely heavily upon normative means requires that most members of the society, most of the time, share a commitment to a set of core values, and that most members, most of the time, will abide by the behavioural implications of these values because they believe in them, rather then being forced to comply with them.
>
> (Etzioni 1997: 13)

These shared values are quite different from intellectual positions that have been agreed after debate or negotiation. They are values that have been 'internalized'; that is, they have become part of the person and have been incorporated into his or her inner self and help to shape his or her preferences. These values have also to be embedded in the four social formations that shape behaviour: the family, the school, the community and the wider community of communities. These social formations constitute what Etzioni calls the moral infrastructure.

The role that Etzioni envisages this moral infrastructure can play in sustaining a normative social order reflects the assumptions he makes about human nature. Almost inevitably, he suggests that communitarian thinking rests upon a 'third view', which is distinct from both the liberal assumption that human nature is essentially benign and capable of being perfected and the conservative assumption that it is brutish and in need of restraint and direction. This 'third view' is a 'dynamic' or 'developmental' one. 'It holds that people are indeed born basically savage' but that they can 'become much more virtuous' (p. 165). Quite how virtuous they can become will depend on the extent to which values are internalized and embedded in the moral infrastructure.

There is, however, a further constraint. Societies that rely upon voluntary commitment must be responsive to the realities of human nature. They cannot espouse 'heroic moral agendas' which ask too much of both individual citizens and the moral infrastructure (p. 174). Within this 'particular limit', however, the social formations have the potential to transform the 'barbarian at birth' into the communitarian citizen.

Much of *The New Golden Rule* is taken up with an extended and sometimes abstract account of how the moral infrastructure can reinforce the character of individuals (p. 187). The key mechanism through which this reinforcement takes place is what Etzioni terms the 'moral voice'. By this he means a 'peculiar form of motivation' that 'encourages people to adhere to values to which they subscribe'. 'The term moral voice is particularly appropriate because people "hear" it. Thus, when a person who affirms a value is tempted to ignore it . . . he or she hears a voice that urges him or her to do what is right' (p. 120). The moral voice has two sources: the external or communal voice and the inner voice. The latter affords a 'special sense of affirmation' when someone adheres to his or her values, and of 'disquiet' when he or she does not. This is, of course, very close to James Q. Wilson's depiction of the moral senses, and, like Wilson, Etzioni believes that the balanced individual is 'doomed to a struggle between a higher and a lower' self (p. 170).

All of this leaves open the question as to what the source of these core values is. From where do they derive their authority and legitimacy? What happens if the values that are internalized and embedded within a particular community conflict with those of another community, or of the wider society of which they are both part? Is what constitutes virtuous behaviour always relative to time and place, or are there criteria against which it is possible to judge one set of values to be superior to another?

These are questions that Etzioni discusses at some length in *The New Golden Rule*, and this discussion cannot be repeated here. In essence, he claims that it is possible to escape from the 'maze of relativism' by identifying two basic virtues that are 'morally compelling in and of themselves'. These are 'a voluntary moral order' and a 'strong measure of bounded individual and sub-group autonomy' (p. 241). These virtues are universal. They are self-evident and have the same status as life and health in the medical sciences. This makes it possible to hold that, for example, racist values, customs and practices are immoral because they are incompatible with the basic virtues, even though they may be widely affirmed within a particular community.

The identification of these basic virtues may allow Etzioni to escape the relativist maze, but it does not in itself resolve the key issues of welfare policy. Particularly important here is the standing of equality or social justice. Etzioni argues that a 'high degree of inequality' is incompatible with both individual autonomy and a voluntary moral order, and that some measure of social justice is a corollary of these basic virtues. The question, however, is what measure? How much equality is needed for a communitarian society? At what point do redistributive measures start to undermine rather than enhance the basic virtues?

Communitarians have given very different answers to these questions, and this diversity can be illustrated by a brief discussion of two recent but contrasting contributions to the communitarian literature: by Jonathan Sacks and by Phillip Selznick.

Jonathan Sacks: welfare and commitment

Jonathan Sacks is the Chief Rabbi of the Hebrew Congregation of the Commonwealth. His book *The Politics of Hope* is not, however, a religious book, nor is it addressed primarily to Jews. What it offers is an eloquent and often impassioned restatement of the communitarian themes already outlined, and a discussion of their application to welfare policy and the family in Britain.

Like Etzioni and Wilson, Sacks believes that the demoralization of Western societies has occurred not because the members of those societies have lost their moral sense, but because it has been stifled by the erosion of the 'institutions which sustain it and the language in which it is expressed' (Sacks 1997: 16). Issues of morality have been 'excluded from polite conversation', and concerns at the weakening of the social fabric dismissed as a moral panic.

Sacks claims that 'two things of great significance occurred around the middle of the twentieth century':

By comparison with previous ages, the state entered the welfare arena and exited the domain of the enforcement of morality. Whether these two opposed and contrary movements are connected or not, they amount to fundamental change in the terms of the social contract.

(p. 115)

The 'nationalisation of responsibility' all but eliminated moral principles from social policy. The role of government became essentially 'procedural'. It was to assess claims, determine entitlement and provide benefits and services – all without reference to the character of those who received them.

Increasingly, welfare came to be administered without preconditions. Any attempt to distinguish between, say, married and unmarried parents, or the unfortunate and the improvident, was an unwarrantable act of judgementalism on the part of government.

(p. 119)

At the same time, the 'privatisation of morality' reduced the role of government to the protection of individual choice. Morality was no longer about the virtues which individuals possess, but about the lifestyle they prefer to lead and the values they choose to adopt.

Sacks argues that these changes can and must be reversed by a new politics of responsibility which 'would establish, through both law and social policy, clearer connections between rights and responsibilities, effort and reward, punishment and blame, action and consequence' (p. 233). An alternative interpretation of such a politics of responsibility has been put forward by Phillip Selznick.

Phillip Selznick: welfare and inclusion

Reference has already been made to Phillip Selznick's defence of communitarian liberalism, and especially of the idea of a common good. These arguments were set out most fully in his major book, *The Moral Commonwealth* (1992). In a more recent essay, however, he has sought to reaffirm the communitarian commitment to social justice and to argue that social justice is a communitarian imperative.

The essay begins by acknowledging that communitarianism's 'chief prescription' is the need for enhanced responsibility in 'every aspect of personal experience and social life'. This, he believes, has 'hit the right note'. He remains 'troubled', however, by the 'selective concern' of some communitarians with 'personal responsibility, personal virtues, personal morality'.

While these themes are music to the ears of conservative writers and politicians ... they pay little attention to the responsibilities of the affluent, or of business leaders. Most important, the moral responsibilities of the community as a whole are given short shrift.

(Selznick 1998b: 61)

Communitarians do not shrink from recognizing that there is plenty of truth in the conservative critique of modern culture. They part company with conservatives, however, insofar as they also look to collective responsibility, and understand that these collective responsibilities include obligations of care for the vulnerable and the disadvantaged.

The crucial point for Selznick, however, is that the responsibilities of the individual and the collectivity are interlinked and in some sense interdependent. 'Personal responsibility', he argues, 'is most likely to flourish when there is genuine opportunity to participate in communal life.' The creation of these opportunities requires substantial investment by the community and its institutions. At the same time, the capacity and the willingness of the community to undertake such investment depends upon the willingness of individuals to accept some measure of personal responsibility for the common good. Communitarians favour progressive taxation because they believe that those who benefit the most should also contribute the most.

This does not mean, however, that communitarians are egalitarians. They do not support the redistribution of resources for its own sake, but in order to prevent social exclusion.

> There is no question of requiring those who have more to help those who have less *just because they have less*. The obligation is owed to people who suffer or who are degraded because they are oppressed and impoverished; to people who are in danger of being despised and excluded – that is, rejected as objects of moral concern.
>
> (Selznick 1998b: 64)

It is this last point which is fundamental to communitarian thinking about equality. Selznick believes that the essence of a flourishing community is that it respects and protects the integrity of its members. It is this understanding, he argues, that 'bridges Biblical and Enlightenment thought'.

> All persons have the same intrinsic worth. They are unequal in many ways – in talents, in contributions, in authority, in power, in valid claims to rewards and resources. But no person's well-being is inherently more worthy of consideration than any other's. Everyone who is a person is equally an object of moral concern.
>
> (p. 63)

This is, of course, very similar to Tawney's argument – discussed in Chapter 1 – that everyone is entitled to an 'equality of respect'. What is important here is the way in which Selznick goes on to argue that social justice requires a 'regime in which everyone's basic needs for life, health, liberty, and hope are respected and addressed'. It follows that communitarians must be committed to a 'baseline equality of condition'. This baseline should be conditional upon the reciprocal exercise of personal responsibility, but it still constitutes a compelling obligation upon the community as a whole.

It will be seen in Chapter 7 that there are striking resonances between Selznick's formulation of communitarian social justice and the rhetoric of Britain's New Labour government. This is especially true of his discussion of the role of self-interest. 'As a communitarian', he writes, 'I have no problem with the idea that self-preservation and self-enhancement are reliable if limited sources of moral ordering.' What the pursuit of social justice requires is not the blinkered denial of self-interest, but a move from 'raw, narrow, short term self interest to broader, more prudent, more long-run conceptions of what rationality requires' (p. 66). It is this kind of rationality, Selznick suggests, that underpins reciprocal and cooperative behaviour, and which can be harnessed to support a strategy of social inclusion.

Communitarianism and welfare reform

It was acknowledged at the beginning of this chapter that the writers discussed here do not focus on welfare issues as specifically as those considered earlier. Even so, it is not hard to identify the central themes of what may be loosely termed a communitarian approach to welfare.

The first and most obvious is an emphasis upon the obligations as well as the rights of those who claim welfare. As the Responsive Communitarian Platform declared, 'the idea of reciprocity' is 'at the heart of the communitarian understanding of social justice' (RCP 1998: xxxiv). In practice this means that welfare benefits should be conditional. An individual's entitlement must depend upon the fulfilment of specified conditions regarding behaviour, whether as a parent, a neighbour or a member of the labour force. Support for such conditionality is not, of course, confined to communitarians, and it is often expressed in terms of a contract – if the government fulfils its side of the bargain by providing services, then claimants should fulfil their side of the bargain by making good use of those services. For communitarians, however, these obligations are much broader and more deeply rooted. They reflect the fact that individuals are not autonomous selves but are socially embedded in communities. At bottom, Selznick argues, responsibilities arise from social involvements or commitments. 'Our lives touch others in many ways, for good or ill, and we are accountable for the consequences' (Selznick 1998b: 62). In Sacks's more dramatic phrase, we 'owe duties to others because they are a part of who we are' (Sacks 1997: 62).

A second theme is the need to build popular support for welfare. This reflects communitarianism's commitment to a voluntary moral order, and its assumption that effective communities can only be created through what the Responsive Communitarian Platform called 'genuine public conviction' (RCP 1998: xxxv). A government that followed a communitarian agenda would have to eschew 'heroic agendas'. Rather than expect too much of the voters, it would have to go to great lengths to appeal to their prudent self-interest and to persuade them that everyone benefited from a welfare system which recognized and served the common good.

A third theme is that welfare must be judgemental and moralistic. Communitarians reject the non-judgementalism of Titmuss and the quasi-Titmuss paradigm on the grounds that it stifles the moral voice. Etzioni, for example, argues in *The New Golden Rule*:

> While social system factors are always important, and sometimes dominate the situation, when they are used to imply that victims have no choice in the matter, which exempts the actors from moral responsibility for their acts, the notion becomes highly damaging to the moral voice.
>
> (Etzioni 1997: 137)

Above all, communitarian welfare would not take people as it found them, but would try to change them. It would seek to shape their values and mould their characters. In Sacks's words, it would employ 'a wider repertoire of policies than those which rely exclusively on coercive legislation, economic incentive, or direct government control'. Instead, it would focus on 'character and on the institutions that promote a strong sense of personhood and social concern' (Sacks 1997: 257).

Conclusion: the limits of persuasion?

Communitarianism shares with paternalism the belief that a central objective of welfare is to enforce social norms and expectations. Where the two perspectives differ sharply is over the methods by which welfare should seek to do this. It was noted at the end of Chapter 3 that the paternalist perspective is essentially a short-term strategy. It is prepared to exercise control and direction over the lives of poor people in order to force them to change their behaviour. Even its staunchest advocates, however, acknowledge that they can offer no assurance that any change in behaviour will be maintained once this direction has stopped. In contrast, the communitarian perspective is a strategy for the longer term. It seeks to persuade people to change their behaviour through moral arguments expressed by and on behalf of the community. Even its staunchest advocates, however, acknowledge that the requisite changes in the moral infrastructure will take time. This is why the present chapter has devoted so much attention to debates about the possibility of a voluntary moral order and about the existence of a moral sense. It is the strength or weakness of moral sentiments that will determine how far communitarian welfare can persuade people to fulfil their obligations and affirm their duties.

A further reason for examining the communitarian perspective on welfare is that it has been a major influence upon New Democrats in the USA and New Labour in Britain. Before discussing this influence, however, there is one further perspective to consider. This is a perspective that has been developed in response to the impact upon the American welfare debate of the arguments about dependency that have been discussed so far. As Steve Teles has explained, these ideas 'opened intellectual space not only on the right but on the left as well, by making it difficult to avoid the fundamental quandaries of social policy' (Teles 1996: 148). By far the most interesting and influential discussions of these quandaries was provided by David Ellwood, whose work is the focus of the following chapter.

Further reading

The best introduction to communitarian thinking is the collection of essays edited by Etzioni (1998). Other good sources are the journal *The Responsive Community* and the Responsive Communitarian Platform website, www.gwu.edu/~ccps. Etzioni (2000) provides a communitarian interpretation of the third way debate. The links between communitarianism and Christian socialism are evident in the volume of essays edited by Askonas and Frowen (1997). James Q. Wilson's thinking about the moral sense and the role of character is developed further in another volume of his essays (1995). The communitarian prescription for welfare and the family is criticized by Levitas (1998) and Stacey (1998). The differences between libertarian and communitarian analyses are highlighted in the exchange between Charles Murray and Melanie Phillips (in Murray 2001).

chapter

five

Welfare as temporary support

The perspective that is explored in this chapter starts from the premise that poverty can never be alleviated by the payment of cash benefits alone. 'Humane welfare', writes David Ellwood (1988: 237), 'will never be realized; too many suspicions and conflicts are built into the system.' The only way to avoid such conflicts, he argues, is to redefine welfare as temporary or transitional assistance. Cash benefits should be provided for a limited period, during which time the recipients will receive education and training. At the end of the period they would be expected to have found work, or, if not, then to take a job in the public sector. Once in work they would become eligible for a range of supplementary benefits and services that would guarantee that their income was higher than they had previously received on welfare and above the poverty line.

According to this perspective, then, a viable system of welfare has three essential features. The first is that cash assistance is temporary. In Ellwood's phrase, 'the long-term support system is jobs' (1988: 181). The second is that work pays, and this in turn requires both new measures to supplement low wages and a radical reform of the system for collecting child support payments from absent fathers. The third is that welfare be understood as a contract between government and claimants. Governments can only require claimants to work if they have first provided adequate training, education and job placement programmes. Claimants can only demand cash assistance if they are prepared to make the most of the opportunities created by these programmes.

By far the clearest and most powerful argument for such a restructuring of welfare was provided by David Ellwood's *Poor Support*, which was published in 1988. Ellwood's book had less to say about the form that such a restructuring should take than it did about the values and 'expectations of our society and its citizens' that should underpin it (p. 9). Even so, *Poor Support* did not draw upon assumptions about human nature and human motivation as explicitly or as fully as did the perspectives discussed in the previous four chapters. In this respect, Ellwood's ideas provide a link between those four chapters and the two that follow. Indeed, it will be seen in these later chapters that his book had a considerable impact upon the welfare reform debate in the USA, and that there are striking parallels between his ideas and those of the New Labour government in Britain.

David Ellwood

David Ellwood had already established a reputation as a leading liberal commentator on welfare by the time that *Poor Support* was published in 1988. An economist, he had first worked on unemployment among African American men, and by the mid-1980s had emerged as a prominent critic of Charles Murray. Indeed, it was seen in Chapter 2 that he had done more than anyone to undermine Murray's original argument that it was the increasing generosity of welfare that had fuelled the growth of lone parenthood. This challenge to Murray, however, was itself grounded in Ellwood's earlier and arguably more significant work on the so-called dynamics of welfare. It will be seen that Ellwood's pioneering development of dynamic analyses informed much of his subsequent writings. Moreover, it will be shown in Chapter 7 that these techniques of dynamic analysis were adopted by British academics in the 1990s and came to have an important influence upon the development of welfare policy in the UK. It is with these analyses of welfare dynamics that the chapter begins, before examining the arguments presented in *Poor Support* itself.

Welfare dynamics

Readers of this book will be all too aware that a central issue in the welfare debates of the early 1980s was the possible impact of benefits upon behaviour. The question that recurred again and again was this: to what extent did the experience of claiming welfare lead people to slacken their efforts to find a job or to re-establish a relationship? Did welfare provide invaluable assistance for short periods or did it ensnare recipients into long-term dependency?

However often the question was asked, and however much acrimony it raised, it was not one that could be answered on the information which was then available. The existing studies of poverty or of welfare dependency drew upon surveys or administrative data. These provided a snapshot of the situation at the time when the survey was conducted or when the statistics were compiled. It was possible to estimate how many households were living on a poverty income or were receiving welfare at that particular time. It was not possible to track those households to see what happened to them in subsequent months or years. Repeating the survey or compiling later statistics would provide another snapshot, another count of households on welfare or in poverty. But they would not necessarily be the same households. The people who were poor or on welfare in 1980, for example, might or might not be the people who were poor or on welfare in 1975 or 1970. This kind of 'snapshot' data, then, could reveal little about the length of time people were in poverty or on welfare, and could not shed light on the extent to which people moved into or out of poverty over time.

This information can be obtained only through longitudinal or panel studies. These studies do re-interview the same respondents, usually at intervals of about a year. Such panel data were becoming available in the USA in the 1980s from the Panel Study of Income Dynamics (PSID), which had begun in 1968 with a panel of 5,000 families and single adults. Working with Mary Jo Bane, Ellwood provided an analysis of the results of PSID (Bane and Ellwood 1994). The mathematics involved were formidable, but Ellwood and Bane were able to identify the events – or 'triggers' – which most commonly preceded moves on to or off welfare, and the personal characteristics and circumstances most strongly associated with long-term dependency.

Their most striking finding was that both sides of the welfare debate were right. Indeed, Ellwood and Bane's early results seemed to defy common sense. On the one hand, the great majority of people who claimed welfare did so for short periods: over half of all 'spells' on welfare lasted less then two years. On the other hand, the bulk of those receiving welfare at any one time would continue to claim it for long periods: over half of current recipients would remain on welfare for more than ten years. Similarly, most claimants were short term, but most welfare expenditures went on long-term claimants.

Ellwood and Bane explained these paradoxes by analogy with a hospital. An observer sitting in the outpatients clinic would deduce that most people using the hospital did so for a short time. Another observer walking round the wards would conclude that many patients would remain for a long period. Both observers would be correct. They were describing different facets of the hospital. Moreover, since someone who was a patient for a year consumed – other things being equal – 52 times as many resources as someone who was there for a week, it followed that most spending went on long-term care even though most patients were short term. Even more significantly, a census conducted on one particular night would capture most of the long-term patients but only a small proportion of the short-term patients. Such a census or sample, then, would be highly unrepresentative of those using the hospital over a year.

All of this was equally true of the welfare system. The 'sterility of debates over welfare', and the 'weakness of much policy making', Bane and Ellwood

(1994: 29) argued, 'can be directly traced to the inability of people' to understand this dual role of welfare. Welfare, they wrote,

is not a drug that ensnares the vast majority of people who ever avail themselves of welfare support. For most, welfare is a short-term transitional program. But for a smaller number, spells can be quite long. And these long-termers represent a very large proportion of the recipients at any one time. Because long-term recipients are a large proportion of the caseload, they receive a roughly equivalently large proportion of the dollars we spend on welfare.

(p. 36)

It will be remembered that most of those receiving welfare were single mothers and their children, and the central issue for policy was how to identify in advance those women who were about to remain on welfare for a long time. There were in fact three characteristics that were associated with long-term receipt of welfare: having never married, having dropped out of school and having little or no work experience. It followed that the women who were most at risk of dependency were those who were disproportionately likely to have all three characteristics – teenage mothers.

Perhaps more surprising was the fact that the majority of claims for welfare were 'triggered' by changes in the family. 'Simply put', Bane and Ellwood wrote, 'AFDC spells almost always begin with a relationship change' (p. 54). Two-fifths start when a divorced, separated or never married woman has a child, and a further two-fifths are triggered by the dissolution of a two-parent family. 'Only 7 percent begin after a decrease in earnings.' Similarly, Bane and Ellwood estimated that only 40 per cent of exits from welfare were due to a rise in earnings (pp. 56–8).

Nevertheless, the central point remained the way in which the 'heterogeneity of the welfare caseload' highlighted 'the overly simplistic stereotyping of both liberals and conservatives' (p. 60). It was absurd to hold welfare responsible for the various social problems that so worried Americans. It was just as absurd, however, to absolve it from all blame. There was a problem of welfare dependency and tackling that problem would be the key to welfare reform.

In the mid-1980s, however, Ellwood was cast in the role of defending welfare against the criticisms of conservatives such as Charles Murray. As he recounted in *Poor Support*, this 'message didn't sell very well'.

People hated welfare no matter what the evidence. It wasn't just conservatives: liberals also expressed deep mistrust of the system, and the recipients themselves despised it. Each group disdained it for different reasons, but the frustration and anger with the present system were unmistakable.

(Ellwood 1988: x)

Ellwood went on to argue that this hostility to welfare did not reflect either a lack of compassion for the poor or a misunderstanding of how welfare functioned. The real problem was much more deep rooted. It was that the rules and regulations that determined eligibility for welfare were trying to strike a balance between goals and values which were inherently non-negotiable. In its current form welfare brought the central values of American society – work, autonomy, responsibility and family – into conflict with each other.

> We want to offer financial support to those with low incomes, but if we do we reduce the pressure on them and their incentive to work. We want to help people who are not able to help themselves but then we worry that people will not bother to help themselves. We recognize the insecurity of single-parent families but, in helping them, we appear to be promoting or supporting their formation. We want to target our money to the most needy but, in doing so, we often isolate and stigmatize them.
>
> (Ellwood 1988: 6)

It was these contradictions which explained why Ellwood found it so hard to counter Murray's arguments. However dubious some of his statistics, however impractical his prescriptions for policy, Murray's work still struck a chord because it highlighted dilemmas that had long been ignored by the liberals. 'Murray', Ellwood wrote, 'is almost certainly correct in stating that welfare does not reflect or reinforce our most basic values. He is also correct in stating that no amount of tinkering with benefit levels or work rules will change that' (p. 6). The question, then, was whether or not welfare could be reformed in a way that met these criticisms rather than simply jettisoned, as Murray proposed.

Poor Support

The central argument put forward in *Poor Support* was that America's welfare system was beyond reform. 'Long-term cash-based welfare for the healthy is inherently flawed' (Ellwood 1988: 237). It was flawed because by providing money and not services, education or training, it treated 'the symptoms of poverty, not the causes'.

> People are not poor just because they lack money. They are poor because they do not have a job, because their wages are too low, because they are trying to raise a child single-handedly, or because they are undergoing some crisis. Worse yet, in treating the symptoms rather than the causes of poverty, welfare creates inevitable conflicts in incentives and values that undermine the credibility and effectiveness of the system.
>
> (p. 7)

Ellwood went on to formulate these conflicts as three 'helping conundrums'. The first and most obvious was the security–work conundrum: the more generous welfare became the less the pressure on those who received it 'to work and care for themselves' (p. 19). The second, the assistance–family structure conundrum, was equally 'transparent': the poverty of single parents had to be relieved, 'yet such aid creates a potential incentive for the formation and perpetuation of such families' (p. 21). It was the third conundrum, however, which Ellwood suggested 'may be the most important of all' (p. 23). This was the targeting–isolation conundrum, and Ellwood's account of it illustrates the ways in which his approach drew upon sharply conflicting perspectives. In part it simply restated Titmuss's warning that targeting 'can label and stigmatize people', but it also echoed Murray's claim that welfare eroded popular support for the behaviours which enabled people to escape from poverty. 'The more attention paid to those who fail, the less seems to be the reward to those who suceed. The danger is that the traditional routes to success lose both their status and their appeal' (p. 24).

There was nothing that was new about Ellwood's depiction of the individual conundrums. What was striking, however, was the way in which he linked them together to argue that any attempt to abolish poverty by providing cash assistance was bound to fail. As soon as benefits approached an adequate level, the conundrums would intensify and the attempt would have to be abandoned. This 'catch-22' could be avoided only by replacing cash assistance with a 'system that ensures that everyone who exercises reasonable responsibility can make it without welfare' (p. 11).

Ellwood's starting point was that for most people 'making it' would mean taking a job. There were, therefore, two issues that had to be resolved in order to devise a viable alternative to welfare. First, what level of paid employment could reasonably be expected of people with differing caring responsibilities? Second, what policies would ensure that those who fulfilled these expectations would be lifted out of poverty?

Ellwood's answer to the first question was that if there were two parents in the family then between them they should hold the equivalent of one full-time full-year job. In the case of single parents, the norm should be half-time work, although mothers with very young children or those with nearly grown children 'might be viewed differently' (Ellwood 1988: 137). His response to the second question was to propose an expansion of in-work benefits, a more rigorous approach to the obligations of absent parents and the recasting of welfare as transitional assistance.

Making work pay

It is important to emphasize at this point that the scope of *Poor Support* was significantly broader than that of Murray's *Losing Ground* or Mead's *Beyond Entitlement*. Neither Murray nor Mead had much to say about the problems of the working poor. They had focused almost exclusively upon the welfare dependent, and had taken it as read that anyone who held down a regular job would not be poor, all the more so if they were living in a two-parent household. They could readily justify this assumption by pointing to the statistics. Not only was the poverty rate among working two-parent families relatively low at around 6 per cent in 1984, but the poverty which was experienced by such families was usually short term (Murray 1987).

From Ellwood's perspective, however, any attempt to solve the problems of welfare had to start with this group. It was true that the working poor were a small proportion of all two-parent families, but they still contained around a quarter of America's poor children. Moreover, these were the people who were 'playing by the rules' but 'losing the game' (Ellwood 1988: 125). They had accepted responsibility for their families and they had found work. They could not, however, earn enough to keep their families out of poverty. Nor did they get much help from the welfare system. They did not receive free medical insurance as they would if they were claiming AFDC, and the only cash benefit available to them was food stamps. Not only did this lack of provision send exactly the wrong signal to the working poor themselves, but it also constituted an unattractive prospect for anyone on welfare.

Ellwood put forward a 'simple' if scarcely inexpensive plan to help the working poor that included the extension of medical coverage through a last-resort government scheme, an increase in the minimum wage and an expansion of the Earned Income Tax Credit (EITC). This last measure is a somewhat complex benefit that provides lower-paid workers with additional tax credits for every dollar they earn. The effect is thus to boost the value of earnings up to a maximum, after which the credits are gradually withdrawn.

The details of Ellwood's plan, however, were far less important than its political purpose. By definition, the working poor did not conform to Mead's picture of a dysfunctional underclass. In Murray's terms they were the 'chumps' who were doggedly working to support their families despite all the perverse incentives generated by welfare. Yet they were not being rewarded. Only a government that ensured that those who worked would not be poor could solve the problems of welfare.

Enforcing child support

The principle that anyone who acted responsibly should be able to avoid recourse to welfare also underpinned Ellwood's proposals on child support. It was noted earlier that his plan for welfare reform rested on the assumption that a lone mother could reasonably be expected to work half-time. When in work she would benefit from the higher minimum wage and enhanced EITC available to all low-paid workers, supplemented by a further tax credit for child care. Even with these improvements, however, a lone mother would not be able to keep her family out of poverty by working half-time. She would need a further source of income, which would have to be outside of welfare and which she could augment with earnings and tax credits. The 'obvious place to look for that help' was the father of her children. In reality, however, the system of child support that was in place in 1988 was 'a disgrace'. The proportion of women who reported receiving payments ranged from just over half of divorced women to around one-quarter of separated women to only one in ten of never married women. Moreover, many of the payments were 'incredibly small', representing only a small fraction of the probable incomes of the fathers (Ellwood 1988: 163).

Children in single-parent families, then, would always be at an 'insurmountable disadvantage' unless a way could be found to force their fathers to recognize their responsibilities. This could be done by ensuring that the birth certificate include the names and social security numbers of both parents, by establishing a universal formula with which to calculate an absent father's payments and by collecting these payments through employers in the same way as social security taxes. Not only would this provide a stable income for many lone mothers, but it could also be expected to have a salutary effect upon the attitudes and behaviour of young men. The obvious drawback was that such a programme would take time to establish and, even when operational, would not remove entirely the need for welfare. It would not be possible to identify and locate every father, and in some cases the amounts collected would be less than the welfare already being paid to the mothers.

There was, however, a 'simple but effective way' to eliminate welfare. This was for the government to augment the money that was collected from the father where this was necessary to bring it up to an adequate amount. Under a scheme of so-called Child Support Assurance first proposed by Irwin Garfinkel, the government would guarantee a minimum level of child support and assume responsibility for pursuing non-paying fathers. Ellwood further proposed that this guarantee be fixed at a level equivalent to half the poverty line for the family. Taken together with his other proposals this would mean that a mother who worked half-time for at least the minimum wage would have an income sufficient to keep her and her children out of poverty. A further advantage was that the child support payments would be clearly distinguished from welfare because they were being made to all lone mothers, not just those who were poor. 'Indeed, most of the money collected would go to middle class women. There would be no stigma, no failure, and no isolation under this system' (Ellwood 1988: 169).

The effect of Ellwood's proposals thus far would have been to ensure that no lone mother need stay poor or on welfare if she were willing to work. The number of hours she would need to work would depend upon her responsibilities, but the fulfilment of her particular obligations would guarantee an income above the poverty line. Such a lone mother would have a powerful incentive to increase her earnings still further, would be no better off as a single parent than in a two-parent family and would be free from the isolation and stigma of welfare. In short, the conundrums would no longer apply to her.

All of this, however, presupposed that she could and would find a job. It would do nothing to help her if she remained on welfare. Ending the scandal of the working poor might send the right signals to those on welfare, but it would not solve the problem of those who could not or would not respond to them.

Transitional assistance

Ellwood's solution to the problem of welfare dependency was to replace welfare with transitional assistance. As its name suggests, transitional assistance would be temporary and Ellwood's advocacy of what came to be called time limits was by far the most controversial aspect of *Poor Support*.

Ellwood argued that time limits were essential if assistance was to avoid the conundrums. He had already established that cash-based welfare could not provide an income above the poverty line without undermining work incentives, threatening the two-parent family and reducing the returns to responsible behaviour. It followed from this that the only route out of poverty for a healthy adult of working age was work; or, at least, work commensurate with his or her caring responsibilities. This in turn meant that any system of welfare should have the clear and unambiguous goal of facilitating this transition to work. The objective should be to enable those receiving cash assistance to acquire the skills and attitudes they needed to get a job, and then to make sure that they took it. This would be undermined if those recipients had the option of remaining on benefit indefinitely. Greater financial incentives were essential, but they would not be sufficient on their own.

> It may seem harsh or unfair to offer only transitional assistance followed by jobs. One could implement the child support assurance plan, medical protection, and the proposals to make work pay without altering the current welfare system. But unless we replace the welfare system, we will not solve the problem that there is little aid, incentive, or pressure for single parents to work. We will not really have avoided the conundrums.
>
> (Ellwood 1988: 180)

Ellwood's specific proposal, then, was that anyone who had 'come on hard times' should apply for 'transitional aid'.

> They would be offered a wide choice of services and could get a cash stipend while they were not working. The services could range from job matching to vocational training to social services to child care. But the

program would be strictly transitional; after some period at least the cash assistance would come to an end.

(p. 123)

Anyone who had not found work at the end of this period would be offered a minimum wage job in the public sector. If they refused that then they would be off benefit and would not be eligible to reapply until they had worked for a period of one or two years.

It will be clear from the discussion thus far that there are obvious commonalties between the positions of Ellwood and Mead. Both men believe in the centrality of paid work, and both believe that the welfare system should offer a combination of what Mead calls 'help and hassle' and what Ellwood describes as 'help and pressure for women to achieve real independence through their own efforts' (1988: 181). Both are prepared to withhold assistance from those who fail to accept their responsibilities.

Nevertheless, the differences between them are real and important. First, Ellwood is not a paternalist as that term was used in the previous chapter. The pressures on those receiving transitional assistance would be intense, but they would be impersonal. They would know that entitlement to welfare would end on a specific date. In the meantime, however, they would not be required to participate in any particular work or training programme, and would not be subject to the personal supervision that was the hallmark of paternalism. Indeed, Ellwood claimed that there was 'not a shred of evidence to justify the claim that imposed work changes attitudes and expectations for the better' (p. 228). Mead's authoritarianism, he argued, reflected his preoccupation with an urban underclass that constituted only a 'tiny fraction of the poor overall' (p. 189).

The most important difference between Mead and Ellwood, however, lies in their expectations of government. For Ellwood the obligation of claimants to act responsibly was matched by that of governments to provide worthwhile training and educational programmes for those without work and child care, and in-work benefits for those in low-paid jobs. Reforming welfare had to be more than just imposing further burdens upon the poor. It had also to generate hope. This was especially true in respect of the ghetto underclass that so concerned Mead. It was reasonable to expect more of 'ghetto residents', Ellwood argued, but only if those expectations went 'hand in hand with genuine opportunities and alternatives' (p. 229).

Ellwood's insistence that governments must first create these 'opportunities and alternatives' reflects his doubts about the number of jobs that would otherwise be available for those leaving welfare. Like W. J. Wilson, whose criticisms of Mead were discussed in Chapter 3, Ellwood was attempting to formulate a role for welfare that recognized the importance of both individual behaviour and the broader societal forces which shaped that behaviour.

Conclusion

There was little that was new about the individual proposals in *Poor Support*. The prominent journalist Micky Kaus, for example, had previously argued that welfare should be replaced by the offer of a job (Kaus 1986, 1992). Moreover, the idea of time limits had received a powerful endorsement in *The New Consensus of Family and Welfare*, a report by a working group of welfare experts with sharply differing perspectives (Novak 1987). As Ellwood (1988: 226) himself noted, the 'notion of mutual responsibility' had ceased to be 'controversial' by the time *Poor Support* was published. Nor was *Poor Support* strong on the details. Ellwood said little, for example, about the last resort job programme that would be needed – and even less about where he would find the money to fund it or how he would counter the anticipated opposition of trade unions in the public sector.

What made *Poor Support* so important for this book, however, was that it drew upon and integrated ideas that had hitherto been assumed to be mutually exclusive. In so doing it put forward a formulation of the purpose of welfare which was clearly distinct from that of Murray or Mead, but which was much less vulnerable to criticisms from them. Indeed, it was the fact that Ellwood was widely regarded as the leading liberal critic of these conservatives which made his advocacy of transitional assistance so significant. As Weaver has noted, Ellwood 'legitimized among mainstream welfare scholars the idea of putting time limits on cash welfare benefits, albeit with a job guarantee at the end' (Weaver 1998: 370).

It was this integrative quality of Ellwood's ideas that also made them attractive to politicians on both sides of the Atlantic who were seeking a fresh approach to welfare reform. In 1991 one of Ellwood's papers was read by Bruce Read, a speech writer for the then Governor Bill Clinton. Later that year Clinton gave a speech at Georgetown University in which he committed himself to imposing a two-year limit on welfare receipt, and he later adopted much of Ellwood's plan in his own book *Putting People First* (Teles 1996: 135). A little over a year later President Clinton was in the White House having promised to 'end welfare as we know it', and Ellwood was Assistant Secretary for Health and Welfare charged with the task of working out how to do it. The outcome is discussed in the next chapter.

Further reading

The techniques and significance of 'dynamic analyses' of longitudinal data are discussed in the essays contained in Leisering and Walker (1998), and their implications for welfare policy are considered in Walker (1998b) and Deacon (1999). An early statement of the case for time-limited welfare in the British context may be found in Layard and Phillpot (1991), and the debate was reviewed in a report by the House of Commons Employment Committee (1996).

 **PART 2**

Policy debates

chapter

six

Ending dependency? Welfare reform in the United States

Few changes in social policy have been as radical or contentious as those made to the US welfare system in the 1990s. At the heart of these changes was the abolition of 'the right to welfare'. It was explained in the Introduction that in the USA welfare is synonymous with means-tested assistance paid primarily to lone mothers and their children. It may be recalled that this assistance is paid in the form of food stamps and cash benefits, and that for many years the most important programme of cash assistance was Aid to Families with Dependent Children (AFDC). It had always been left to individual states to decide how much they were prepared to pay in AFDC, but all were required by law to pay something to people whose income and resources fell below the limits defined by the federal government. That obligation was lifted by the cumbersomely titled Personal Responsibility and Work Opportunity Reconciliation Act of 1996 (PRWORA), which abolished AFDC and replaced it with a radically different programme called Temporary Assistance for Needy Families (TANF). The relevant part of the Act began with a declaration that it should not 'be interpreted to entitle any individual or family to assistance under any state program funded under this part' (Weaver 2000: 456).

The ending of entitlement was a means to an end. The preamble to the Act set out two central objectives of welfare reform. The first of these was to 'end the dependency of needy parents on government benefits by promoting job preparation, work and marriage'. The second objective was to 'prevent and reduce the incidence of out-of-wedlock pregnancies' and to 'encourage the formation and maintenance of two-parent families' (Duerr Berrick 1998: 5).

The first objective was to be met primarily through the introduction of time limits. States were now debarred from using TANF funds to pay benefits to a family that included an adult who had already claimed welfare for a total of five years during his or her lifetime. They were also to ensure that no one could receive welfare for two years without participating in work activities. The second objective was to be met through a series of provisions which withheld benefits from women who did not meet specific conditions regarding their own behaviour or that of their children. These provisions were reinforced by changes in the way in which welfare was funded. The most important effects of these changes were to offer a significant windfall to states which reduced their caseloads, and to reward states that met targets for the proportion of TANF recipients engaged in work activities or managed to reduce out-of-wedlock births without increasing the number of abortions.

The introduction of TANF was accompanied by other changes that were designed to boost the incomes of people who moved from welfare to work. The Earned Income Tax Credit (EITC) was made more generous, health insurance was extended to the children of low-paid workers and child support payments were to be enforced more vigorously. As Robert Lerman has written, the ending of entitlement, the move to a block grant and the attempts to make work pay were all of a piece. They added up to a 'realignment of US welfare policies' which was 'real, significant, but often misunderstood' (Lerman 1999: 224).

There is now an extensive literature on the nature of this 'realignment' and on its implications for those on welfare and those in low-wage jobs (Bryner 1998; Weaver 2000; Wiseman 2001). This chapter provides a brief overview of this literature. It does so for two reasons. First, and most important, the policy debates of the 1990s illustrate very clearly the ways in which conflicting approaches to welfare reform draw upon the perspectives outlined in this book. Second, it will be seen in the following chapter that American ideas and experiences have been a significant influence upon New Labour thinking on welfare reform in Britain.

Welfare reform and the Clinton administration

It was seen in Chapter 5 that Bill Clinton had adopted many of David Ellwood's ideas and had made welfare reform a central theme of his campaign for the presidency. In January 1993 the newly elected President Clinton created a task force on welfare reform which was to be co-chaired by Ellwood and Bruce Reed, and was also to include Mary Jo Bane.

The omens looked good. There appeared to be a broad consensus both within and between the major parties that reform was inevitable, not least because of its evident popularity with the voters (Weaver 1998: 379; Wiseman 2001: 228). The impetus for reform was reinforced still further by the seemingly remorseless rise in welfare caseloads. The number of families in receipt of AFDC peaked at just over five million in March 1994, a rise of 30 per cent since 1989. These families included over 14 million people – of whom 10 million or two-thirds were children (Bryner 1998: 5–6). One American in 20 was dependent upon welfare in the spring of 1994. In the event, however, the Clinton administration did not produce its welfare plan until June 1994. Shortly after taking office the new administration had decided to give priority to the reform of health care, and the delays this caused were exacerbated by the difficulty of finding the money to pay for welfare reform (Ellwood 1996: 26). These delays were to prove critical because the Clinton plan was designed to consolidate the consensus on welfare that had seemed to be developing in the early 1990s. It did this by combining significant increases in spending on child care, education and training with the introduction of time limits on welfare and a requirement that lone mothers on welfare live with a responsible adult (Bryner 1998: 83). By the time the plan appeared, however, the prospects for building a political coalition in support of reform were bleak.

The change in the political climate was due in part to the growth of opposition to time limits within the Democratic Party. Some Democrats could not accept the idea of denying benefits to poor mothers, even those who refused to work. What Micky Kaus (1986: 26) had derided as 'whistle while you workfare' proved to be surprisingly resilient. Nevertheless, a far more important reason for the collapse of the consensus around welfare was the dramatic shift of opinion that had occurred within the Republican Party. It was seen in Chapter 2 that Charles Murray had come to argue more and more forcefully that the central issue in welfare was not non-work but 'illegitimacy'. He insisted that the introduction of stiffer work requirements into welfare would do little to halt the growth in out-of-wedlock births, and that the only solution was to withhold welfare completely from single mothers.

Steve Teles has described the impact of what he terms 'Murray's ideological stink bomb' (Teles 1996: 157). By early 1994 prominent Republican think tanks were calling for a policy of withholding AFDC and food stamps from new single mothers. Empower America, for example, claimed that the need was not for 'tougher work provisions and job training' but 'to go after a system that fosters illegitimacy and its attendant social pathologies' (p. 152). If a lone mother wished to keep her baby, the argument ran, then she should have to look to her family or private charities for support, or else live in supervised accommodation. One of the most prominent advocates of this position was Robert Rector of the Heritage Foundation, 'who became as influential among Republicans in 1995 as Lawrence Mead was in 1988' (p. 159).

Other conservatives, however, still supported the earlier emphasis upon work, while a further complication was the influence of conservative Christian groups. These bitterly opposed restrictions on welfare, such as the introduction of a family cap, on the grounds that they would encourage poor women to seek an abortion rather than have an additional child (Bryner 1998: 83; Joffe 1998). It is perhaps not surprising, then, that in the midst of all this confusion and acrimony a growing number of politicians and commentators were attracted to the idea of simply leaving it to individual states to resolve the most intractable issues. Moreover, those who advocated such a policy of devolution to the states could point to the success of the so-called waiver programme as evidence that it not just politically convenient but also perfectly feasible.

The waivers

The original purpose of the waiver provision was to allow individual states to experiment with new ways of delivering welfare. Under legislation passed in 1962 a state could submit a proposal for a demonstration project to the Secretary of State together with a request that he waive the federal regulations governing entitlement to benefit where this was necessary for the experiment to proceed. The crucial point was that the decision on whether or not to grant the waiver was taken by the White House, not by Congress. The original legislation had envisaged that the demonstration projects that were facilitated by the waivers would seek ways of making AFDC more successful. After 1986, however, the Reagan and first Bush administrations used waivers to undermine AFDC.[1] Specifically, they encouraged states to attach more conditions to receipt of AFDC and to challenge the idea of an entitlement to welfare.

The first set of waivers allowed states to impose more stringent work conditions than were required by the existing legislation. The first Bush administration, however, encouraged a shift in emphasis towards the regulation of sexual behaviour and the deterrence of illegitimacy. Henceforth waivers were designed primarily to erode the rights to welfare that had been established by a series of judgements of the Supreme Court.

Back in 1968 the Supreme Court had ruled in the celebrated case of *King v. Smith* that a state could not deny welfare to someone who was otherwise eligible on the grounds of her illicit sexual conduct.

> The Court sharply distinguished between attitudes to work which it considered malleable and thus within the bounds of acceptable state regulation, and sexual behaviour, which it treated as innate (and private) and thus beyond the realm of state jurisdiction.
>
> (Teles 1996: 140)

The Bush administration set out to use waivers to negate this and other similar decisions. For its part the subsequent Clinton administration adopted a policy of accepting virtually every waiver request it received. The result was a dramatic change in the nature of the welfare system. By the mid-1990s, 18 states had introduced a family cap; 31 states had made welfare conditional upon satisfactory attendance at school (learnfare); 17 states required teen mothers to live with a parent or guardian; and 21 states withheld welfare from mothers who failed to ensure that their children were immunized or met other health care requirements (Bryner 1998: 201–5). The operation of the waivers thus reflected the influence of the 'new paternalism' upon welfare policy. It also reinforced the political pressures for devolution by persuading many in Washington that welfare 'could simply be handed off to the states' (Teles 1996: 160).

The 1996 Act and its critics

Kent Weaver (2000) has provided a brilliant account of the events which led up to the eventual enactment of PRWORA in August 1996. The turning point was the landslide victory of the Republican Party in the Congressional elections of 1994. Clinton now faced Republican majorities in both the Senate and the House of Representatives. Both the Republicans and Democrats had promised drastic changes in welfare, and both were aware that the public would not forgive them if they failed to deliver on this commitment. Neither, however, would accept reform on the other party's terms. The outcome was that welfare became the focus of ever more complex 'strategic games' (Weaver 1998: 363). Policy initiatives were advanced and resisted by the parties not simply on their merits but on their capacity to embarrass opponents or to divert attention from divisions within their own ranks. This complex manoeuvring was to culminate in Clinton's decision on the eve of the 1996 presidential election to sign into law a Republican Bill that appeared to be much more punitive than his own plan.

It was noted earlier that the new Act ended the 'right to welfare'. There was now to be a limit to the length of time people could receive TANF benefits, and within this time limit states were given much more freedom to formulate their own rules governing eligibility for welfare. It was also noted that the funding of the new programme gave each state a strong financial incentive to reduce the number of families on welfare. In broad terms the federal government in Washington had matched a state's spending on AFDC dollar for dollar. If more families were admitted to welfare, then the federal grant rose accordingly. This meant that welfare was relatively cheap for individual states, and especially for those with the lowest incomes per head, which received proportionately greater funding from the federal government. The 1996 Act replaced this matched funding with an annual lump sum or block grant. This grant was based upon the amount each state had received in 1993 or 1994. If states expanded their welfare caseloads they would have to meet the extra costs; if they reduced their caseloads they would save money.

The new Act also sought to influence the reproductive behaviour of poor women, both through the imposition of conditions upon the women themselves and through the payment of financial bonuses to state governments that met aggregate targets. States, for example, were prohibited from paying TANF to mothers under 18 who did not live with an adult or did not attend school, but were to receive an increase in their block grant if they succeeded in reducing out-of-wedlock births without increasing the number of abortions. There was also to be an additional bonus for the five states that achieved the biggest reduction in their illegitimacy ratios. In addition, all states now had the option of introducing a family cap, and could withhold benefits from mothers who did not help to identify the fathers of their children, did not attend school or had drug convictions. It was seen in Chapter 1 that Daniel Moynihan had provoked uproar in 1965 by talking of a 'tangle of pathology' that threatened to engulf the black family. Now he was dismayed at the assumption that the 'behaviour of certain adults can be changed by making the lives of their children as wretched as possible' (quoted in Bryner 1998: 198).

Nevertheless, the most controversial feature of the new Act was that it did not require state governments to fund work and training programmes for those who came up against the new time limits. This was by far the biggest difference between PRWORA and Clinton's original proposals, and it was the main reason why the President's decision to sign the bill was famously denounced by one of his former aides as 'The worst thing Bill Clinton has done' (Edelman 1997). Another notable critic was David Ellwood, who had earlier resigned from the administration. He condemned the new measures enacted in 1996 as 'appalling'. They offered claimants not 'two years and you work' but two years 'followed by nothing – no welfare, no jobs, no support' (Ellwood 1996: 26). The Nobel Prize winning economist Robert Solow was equally forthright. It would be impossible, he argued, for the labour market to absorb a sudden influx of unskilled and inexperienced women workers, and the result would be a sharp rise in unemployment and a drop in wage rates. There was, then, a widespread expectation among political and academic commentators that what Theda Skocpol (1996: 21) called the 'Shirk Responsibility for the Poor Act' would have dire consequences for the poor. Daniel Moynihan, for example, predicted that it would exclude many people from welfare and 'substantially increase poverty and destitution' (quoted in Bryner 1998: 173).

The impact of reform

The debate over the impact of PRWORA has been as complex as that which surrounded its passage. There is considerable agreement about what has happened, but much less agreement about why it has happened. It is universally accepted that the implementation of PRWORA has coincided with a truly remarkable decline in the welfare caseload. The number of people in receipt of welfare fell by more than half from over 14 million in January

1994 to just under seven million in June 1999 (Weaver 2000: 343). What remains a matter of debate is the extent to which this fall is due to welfare reform, to other measures, such as the expansion of Earned Income Tax Credit, or simply to the extraordinary strength of the US economy in the 1990s. In 1998, for example, the number of people in work rose by nearly three million, the unemployment rate fell to its lowest level since 1969 and the average hourly rate of low-paid workers rose for the first time in two decades (CBPP 1999: 1). Similarly, expenditure on EITC almost doubled in real terms between 1993 and 1999, and by 1999 the total spent on aid to the working poor far exceeded what was spent on the old AFDC programme (Besharov and Germanis 2001: 67).

It is quite probable, then, that the buoyancy of the labour market created jobs for people who had always been keen to work but had hitherto been denied an opportunity to do so. It is equally probable, however, that the reforms pushed some people into accepting jobs that they would not have taken previously. Quite where the balance lies is a matter of interpretation and not something that can be determined on the evidence that is available. What can be said is that it is the interaction of the economy, the reforms and the measures to make work pay that has had such a powerful effect. None of these factors would have had the same impact in isolation from the other two. Robert Lerman, for example, has pointed out that welfare reform has stimulated current and prospective claimants to look for work. The Labour Force Participation ratio for never-married mothers jumped from 60 per cent in 1994 to about 74 per cent in 1998, compared with a rise from 69 to 70 per cent for married mothers. Equally important, however, is the fact that the economy generated jobs for all of the 740,000 never-married mothers who entered the labour force between 1996 and 1998. Indeed, the unemployment rate for this group actually fell from 19 to 15 per cent over the period (Lerman 1999: 237).

This does not mean, of course, that all those who have left welfare are now in paid employment. In fact the decline in the welfare caseload is almost double the increase in the number of working mothers, 2.4 million compared to 1.25 million between March 1994 and March 1999 (Besharov and Germanis 2001: 72). It is unlikely that there has been a sudden rise in non-reported employment, and so nearly half of those who have left welfare must be being supported by a combination of some or all of food stamps, disability benefits, subsidized housing and, most of all, other members of the household. Besharov and Gemanis, for example, point out that under the old AFDC programme nearly one-third of all claimants were living with another adult. They suggest that some of these women had sufficient resources to 'forgo welfare' when 'faced with the new work and behavioural requirements' (p. 74).

Many of those who did choose to 'forgo welfare' in this way would have done so to avoid the hassle that is now part and parcel of claiming TANF benefits. It is not widely appreciated that a relatively small proportion of welfare recipients are engaged in work experience or community service. Although the Act set out targets for the proportion of claimants engaged in work activities, the states are allowed to offset reductions in the caseload against these targets. In addition, the Act allows for a very broad interpretation of the term 'work activities'. As Michael Wiseman has put it, 'there's not much work in American workfare'. The central message is that 'welfare without work will be a hassle. Its not the job you can't refuse; its the appointment you can't refuse' (Wiseman 2001: 43).

All of this helps to explain the seemingly contradictory trends in the data on poverty. The overall poverty rate has declined, albeit much more slowly than the caseload. The proportion of Americans living in poverty declined from 13.7 per cent in 1996 to 12.7 per cent in 1998. Moreover, the Center on Budget and Policy Priorities (CBPP) reported in October 1999 that the proportion of children in poverty was the lowest for 20 years and that both the poverty rate for African Americans and that for the southern states were at an all time low (CBPP 1999: 1). Even this, however, is not the whole story, since those families that remained poor were living in deeper poverty than before. Indeed, on the third anniversary of the passage of the Act the Children's Defense Fund (CDF) claimed that the number of children living in households with an income less than half the poverty line had risen by nearly half a million to 2.7 million between 1996 and 1999. The number of households headed by a single mother who were living in such extreme poverty had increased by 26 per cent over the same period (CDF 1999: 1).

This indicates that the immediate consequence of welfare reform has been a growing bifurcation of the poor in America. Many of those who have remained on welfare have experienced a further decline in their incomes, as have some of those who left welfare without finding work. At the same time, many of those who have moved from welfare to paid employment have been able to escape from poverty, although there remains some dispute over the extent to which they are better off in work (Jencks 1997).

There is, however, one further feature of the 1996 Act which is of great significance. This is that it reflects and reinforces the belief of most Americans that single mothers should look for paid employment, even when their children are very young. As Ann Orloff has pointed out, the Act 'eliminates caregiving as a base for making claims within the US welfare state' (Orloff 2000: 133). TANF provides for a single mother on the grounds that she is a potential worker, not that she is someone with recognized responsibilities for the care of children. Lone mothers may be entitled to assistance with child care if and when they take paid employment, but they can no longer 'maintain a household' without either 'access to a male wage' or themselves 'working for pay' (p. 142). She goes on to argue that the lack of opposition to this change from 'women's equality organizations' reflects the fact that the great majority of married mothers were already in paid work. 'AFDC rules seemed to make possible staying at home to care for children at public expense – exactly what isn't guaranteed to any other mother or father' (p. 152). The same point was made by Hilary Clinton in an interview with *Time* magazine in 1996. She was asked whether 'it makes sense to force a single mother of a young child to work'.

> I've thought about that a lot. I think getting up and going to work, going to school and having to make the same difficult decisions about who cares for your children that every other working mother has to make is a necessary step toward learning how to be self-sufficient. Yes, people who are physically able to work ought to work.
>
> (Sheehy 2000: 289)

The discussion thus far has focused upon the extent to which the Act has succeeded in moving people from welfare to work. This, however, is not its only objective. If anything the welfare reform debates of the 1990s were dominated by fears about the effects of increasing rates of 'illegitimacy' even more than by concerns about the work levels of the poor. In practice, however, states have been far less active in developing new programmes to reduce out-of-wedlock births than they have in promoting work. Indeed, a multi-state analysis of the welfare systems created under the Act found little enthusiasm for or agreement about 'the Act's anti-reproductive and marriage goals' (Gentry *et al.* 1999: 3). In general the study found that state initiatives targeted at non-marital pregnancy were fragmented and lacked a clear focus. 'A case in point: the five states that won the bonus to reward decreases in illegitimacy did not know what they had done to accomplish this, and, in fact, it appeared that at least some of them had done little or nothing at all' (p. 15).

Conclusion

It was noted at the beginning of this chapter that the changes made to the US welfare system in the 1990s were radical and controversial. It should now be added that the early impact of those changes has confounded many of their critics. The reforms have not just helped to halve the numbers dependent upon welfare. They have also increased significantly the Labour Force Participation ratio of single mothers, and this in turn has enabled many to escape from poverty.

There are, however, several reasons why many commentators remain cautious about the long-term consequences of welfare reform. The first is that not enough is known about the circumstances of those who have left welfare, and particularly about the conditions of those who have been subject to sanctions. The second is the fact that the extraordinarily benign economic environment in which the reforms have been implemented could not last forever. Perhaps the most important reason for caution, however, is the simple fact that it will become more difficult to reduce caseloads and to increase work levels in the future. This is because it is those who are the most employable who are the first to leave welfare and those who are the hardest to help who remain on the rolls. It is by no means clear what will happen when these more difficult cases come up against time limits, especially if there has been a downturn in the labour market.

Of more immediate relevance to this book, however, is the way in which the policy debates of the 1990s drew upon the perspectives that were outlined in the earlier chapters. The most obvious and direct influence upon the 1996 Act was David Ellwood's argument that work must pay and that welfare should be recast as transitional assistance. Indeed, the significance of Ellwood's role is reflected in the strength of the attacks made upon him by left-wing academics such as Frances Fox Piven. Back in 1989 she had told Ellwood that time limits would be the only one of his proposals to be adopted (Orloff 1998: 40), and she reacted with fury to his criticisms of the 1996 Act. 'He seems not to understand that he helped unleash the political maelstrom that is producing escalating welfare cutbacks' (Piven 1996: 14).

Another factor that shaped the debates that led up to the passage of the 1996 Act was the conflict within the Republican Party between the authoritarianism of Lawrence Mead and the abolitionism of Charles Murray. In the event it was the new paternalism discussed in Chapter 3 that emerged as the dominant influence upon the design and delivery of TANF. The Republicans in Congress were not prepared to withhold welfare completely from lone mothers and their children. Both they and the Clinton administration, however, were prepared to subject those mothers to much more stringent work requirements and to demand that they accept a greater level of surveillance and direction over their personal lives while they remained on welfare.

The authoritarianism of much of the 1996 Act provides a clear illustration of the importance of ideas. At the same time it must be acknowledged that this approach has been far more successful in promoting paid work than it has been in promoting marriage or in reducing the number of births to teenagers. This is another reason why even the most enthusiastic supporters of the reforms remain uncertain about their effectiveness in the long term (Deacon 2001).

In the final analysis, however, the most striking feature of the policy debates of the 1990s was what was not debated. It is true that some did criticize the overwhelming preoccupation of politicians and commentators with the size of the caseload, and did call for more attention to be given to the numbers in poverty (Wiseman 1999). Hardly anyone, however, challenged the emphasis upon the obligations rather than the rights of claimants, or the priority given to promoting work rather than increasing the rates of benefit. As Kent Weaver has noted, Clinton's pledge to 'end welfare as we know it' had 'implicitly reinforced conservative critiques of welfare' (Weaver 1998:

379). This shift in the focus of the debate has been so complete that it is all too easy to take it for granted, and to fail to appreciate the extent of the change that has taken place since the 1960s and 1970s. It will be seen in the next chapter that much the same can be said of the debate in Britain.

Note

1 The Republican Ronald Reagan was President from 1980 to 1988, and his fellow Republican George Bush was President from 1988 to 1992. The Democrat Bill Clinton served as President from 1992 to 2000, when Republican George W. Bush began his first term.

Further reading

The definitive account of welfare reform in the USA is that of Kent Weaver (1998, 2000), and the impact of reform is discussed from a variety of perspectives by Besharov and Germanis (2001), Deacon (2001), Grant (2000) and Lerman (1999). The response of feminists in the USA is discussed in Orloff (2000). An important restatement of the centre left position on welfare is that of Skocpol (2000). There is a continual stream of research findings and commentaries upon welfare reform posted on the websites of the leading US think tanks and research institutes. The most important of these include the Urban Institute, the Center on Budget and Policy Priorities and the Manpower Demonstration Research Corporation. These sites can all be accessed through the electronic policy network www.epn.org. Another important site is that of the Hudson Institute: www.hudson.org. Articles on welfare reform appear regularly in the magazine *The American Prospect* and this can also be accessed through the electronic policy network.

chapter

seven

A new deal for welfare? New Labour and the reform of welfare in Britain

There are few commentators who would dispute that the election of the New Labour government in May 1997 constituted a significant turning point in British politics. Indeed, there has since been a plethora of academic and journalistic writings on almost every aspect of New Labour. The purpose of this chapter is to discuss New Labour's approach to welfare reform, and in particular to show how that approach draws upon the perspectives outlined in earlier chapters. This, of course, was also the purpose of the previous chapter on policy debates in the USA. Nevertheless, it will be found that the present chapter has a different structure from Chapter 6. This is because the policy debate in Britain is broader and more wide-ranging than it is in the USA. It was explained in the Introduction that the term welfare does not have the same specific meaning in Britain that it does in the USA. Moreover, there has not been in Britain a single measure of welfare reform equivalent to the passage of the 1996 Act in the USA. The closest to the 1996 Act in Britain was the launch of the New Deals, and especially that for young people. The development of the New Deals, however, has been an incremental process, and they are only one of a number of measures that have been introduced over a period of years. It follows that there has not been the same tightly focused debate as there has been in the USA; nor is there the same clear break between 'before' and 'after' welfare reform. All of this means that it is more helpful for the present chapter to examine in turn the four central themes of New Labour's approach to welfare reform:

- the need to strike a new balance between the rights and the obligations of claimants;
- the need to widen access to paid employment and to make such work 'pay';
- the need to rebuild popular support for welfare;

- the need to combat social exclusion and poverty, especially that endured by families with young children.

The chapter also discusses why New Labour has not sought to reduce the role of the means test by anything like as much as may have been anticipated from the discussion of Frank Field's ideas in Chapter 2. Before doing any of these things, however, the chapter considers New Labour's claim that its reform of the welfare state is but one example of a new politics of the centre left – a new politics that it shared with the former Clinton administration in the USA and that both hailed as a 'third way'.

There is, of course, an enormous literature on the 'third way', and much of it is highly critical, even dismissive, of the whole idea. Moreover, the election of a Republican President in the USA is likely to increase still further the already widespread doubts about the interest and value of the third way debate. Even so, the idea of the 'third way' is still very important for this book. There are two reasons for this. The first is that, as will be seen in the following chapter, the broader debate about the nature of the third way has provided a conceptual framework that is extremely helpful in analysing conflicting perspectives on the future of welfare. The second and more immediate reason is that it is necessary to understand what key New Labour figures mean by the third way in order to understand what they are trying to achieve in welfare reform.

A third way for welfare?

The obvious starting point is what might be termed the 'authorized version' of the third way, that put forward by the Prime Minister Tony Blair and the man often described as 'his favourite guru', the sociologist Anthony Giddens. Both believe that the essence of the third way lies in the need to adapt the traditional values of the centre left to contemporary social and economic conditions.

For Giddens the third way is 'a framework of thinking and policy making that seeks to adapt social democracy to a world that has changed fundamentally over the past two or three decades' (Giddens 1998: 26). The essence of his argument is that a new politics is required to 'help citizens pilot their way through the major revolutions of our time: globalization, transformations in personal life, and our relationship to nature' (p. 64). These revolutions have given rise to problems that cut across the old left/right divide, and hence the third way has to 'transcend both old-style social democracy and neo-liberalism' (p. 26). At the same time these revolutions generate new risks that people have to confront in a world in which tradition and custom have become much less important. To a far greater extent than in the past people now have to act as moral agents, they have to decide for themselves what they should do rather than look to the state, religion or established custom and practice. On many issues, then, the third way will involve a search for a 'new relationship between the individual and the community' (p. 65).

Tony Blair also believes that the third way 'stands for a modernized social democracy'. For him, however, modernization is less a matter of adapting to global transformations than of casting aside the polarities of the old politics. According to Blair, the third way does not just split the difference between the old left and the right. Indeed, the defining feature of third way politics is that it 'reconciles themes which in the past have been wrongly regarded as antagonistic'. It does not see a contradiction between the creation of wealth and the pursuit of social justice. It seeks both to promote enterprise and to attack poverty and discrimination (Giddens 1998a: 1).

In the case of welfare this means accepting that a commitment to greater equality is not incompatible with a concern about benefit dependency. It is quite possible, the argument runs, that a small-scale but significant problem of dependency could develop within an increasingly unequal society. The third way, then, recognizes that 'gross inequalities continue to be handed down from generation to generation' and that it is necessary to 'robustly tackle the obstacles to true equality of opportunity' (p. 3). At the same time it must develop policies which focus upon the long-term poor and which require them to accept their own responsibility to make the most of the opportunities that New Labour will create.

These are, of course, big claims and critics have been quick to argue that the third way is an attempt to square circles. Driver and Martell, for example, argue that 'Blair's third way' is trying to 'reconcile what are in the end irreconcilables'. This is because it is

> impossible to synthesise the counterposed options of Left and Right, social democracy, liberalism and conservatism. There are essential and irresolvable tensions between them and their principal values: equality, liberty and authority.
>
> (Driver and Martell 2000: 155)

What it is possible to do, they argue, is to find compromises between these positions, to strike new trade-offs between the different values and principles. Moreover, 'such deals' are made 'at the policy coal-face'. It is within programmes such as the New Deal that New Labour has sought 'some balance or *modus operandi* between the demands of competing political values', and they suggest that it is this 'more pragmatic and limited notion of politics and public policy' that best defines 'any third way' (p. 155).

This is a compelling argument. Nevertheless, it is argued here that the nature of the trade-offs that are made, and the reasons for them, can be understood more fully as an attempt to draw upon and accommodate elements of the conflicting perspectives outlined in this book. It is in this sense that New Labour's 'third way' will be seen to be both more radical and more integrative than Driver and Martell allow.

What is important here is not that New Labour has produced a new combination of incentives, authority and moral exhortation. It is that this new combination represents an attempt to respond to conservative ideas about dependency without abandoning altogether the goal of greater equality. This has led the Blair governments to commit themselves to the elimination of child poverty, while abandoning long established taboos on judgementalism and on discussions of personal behaviour. More than anything else, however, it has led New Labour to emphasize the obligations of claimants.

The enforcement of obligations

Both Blair and Giddens have consistently argued that welfare reform is a centrepiece of third way politics, and that it must involve a 'redefinition of rights and responsibilities' (Giddens 1998: 65). Indeed, Giddens has gone on to suggest that 'a prime motto for the new politics' might be 'no rights without responsibilities' (p. 65). It will be apparent that this represents an important shift in centre left thinking in Britain away from the quasi-Titmuss paradigm discussed in Chapter 1. It will also be apparent that this shift owes much to the influence of American ideas and especially of communitarianism and the new paternalism.

In 1995 Tony Blair delivered a speech entitled 'The Rights We Enjoy Reflect the Duties We Owe'. In it he declared that an incoming Labour government would have two critical objectives: to modernize the economy and to 'move people from welfare to work, eliminating the social evil of welfare dependency'. It would achieve the second objective by combining new opportunities to work with a 'reasonable obligation to take the chances offered'. 'A society geared to extending opportunity is one then able to demand responsibility with some realistic prospect of it being given. It allows us to be much tougher and hard headed in the rules we apply, and how we apply them' (Blair 1995: 7).

Other examples of this tough-minded approach were the introduction of home/school contracts which would set out the obligations of parents in respect of 'attendance and time-keeping, homework and standards', and the requirement that tenants in social housing meet new conditions regarding their behaviour. He insisted that a New Labour government would not be 'squeamish' about passing judgement on people who failed to fulfil their obligations to their immediate neighbours or the wider community in which they lived.

> Families have the right to be housed. But they do not have any right to terrorise those around them, be it with violence, racial abuse or noise.

If tenants do not fulfil their side of the bargain, particularly after repeated warnings, the contract is broken.

(p. 9)

Once in office New Labour did not shrink from introducing a significant element of conditionality into the delivery of welfare. The most important example is, of course, the requirement that young unemployed people participate in the New Deal, and this is discussed further below. The use of compulsion within the welfare to work programme, however, is only one of the ways in which an individual's entitlement to benefits or services is now dependent upon his or her behaviour (Dwyer 1998; Lister 1998; Dwyer and Heron 1999). Moreover, this emphasis upon conditionality is likely to become still more prominent in Labour's second term. In a speech during the election campaign, for example, Tony Blair (2001) reaffirmed his belief that 'active responsibility' should be at the core of welfare reform. He then went on to announce that benefit sanctions would be imposed upon those who lacked basic skills in literacy and numeracy but failed to take the training courses that would be made available.

The rationale for this approach was first set out in full in the consultation document *A New Contract for Welfare*, which the government published in March 1998. This so-called Green Paper was short on policy detail, but it provided an important statement of the government's intentions on welfare. It did so, moreover, in language that echoed almost exactly that which Tony Blair had himself employed in a series of speeches before and after the election (Deacon 1998). The Green Paper spoke, for example, of the need to end a welfare system that 'chains people to passive dependency instead of helping them to realise their full potential' (DSS 1998a: 9). It talked also of the need for services which were 'active', not passive, and which pushed people to 'achieve independence'. The experience of the past 50 years, it claimed, has shown that 'cash hand outs alone can lead to a life of dependency' (p. 71). At the same time the Green Paper rejected the idea that the welfare state could be reduced to a residual safety net for the poor. This, it said, was 'the route to a divided society – one side on benefit, the other paying for it' (p. 19). The answer was, of course, the government's third way – 'a welfare state providing for the mass of the people but in new ways to fit the modern world' (p. 19). The cornerstone of this new welfare state was to be the welfare to work programme. It was this, above all, which would 'break the mould of the old, passive benefits system' (p. 24).

The centrality of paid work

The Green Paper was unequivocal that the government's aim was to 'rebuild the welfare state around work' (DSS 1998a: 23): 'Our ambition is nothing less than a change of culture among benefit claimants, employers and public servants – with rights and responsibilities on all sides' (p. 24). The rationale for this change of culture was simple. For most people of working age the quickest way to escape from poverty is to get a job. In order to do so they need to acquire the skills and capacities that employers now demand. The existing benefit system, however, did not help or encourage them to do so. It had, in the words of a later government document, become 'part of the problem; not the solution' (DSS 1999a: 29).

This had been the central message of the Borrie Commission, an informal Commission set up by Blair's predecessor John Smith to inform Labour thinking on social and economic policy. The Commission's report had dismissed the arguments of those it termed the levellers that 'redistribution through taxes and benefits must be the basis of social justice, and that we cannot rely on paid work to haul the poor out of poverty' (Borrie Commission 1994: 112). Instead it had extolled the strategy of the investors, for whom 'social justice is pursued primarily through investment in opportunities (rather than simply supporting the non-employed on benefits)' (p. 97). What is needed, it said, was 'a revolution in welfare to enable people to earn their way out of poverty' (p. 224).

At the time the Commission's emphasis upon paid work owed more to its scepticism regarding the willingness of the British taxpayer to fund more generous benefits than it did to any optimism regarding prospects for the labour market. Its arguments, however, were strengthened by the findings of the early studies of income dynamics in Britain. The basis of so-called dynamic analyses was discussed in Chapter 5. In essence they draw upon the results of panel surveys which interview the same people year on year. This makes it possible to track the incomes of people over time, and to identify the events or triggers that lead to significant changes in those incomes. The most important source of such panel data on incomes in Britain is the British Household Panel Survey (BHPS), which began in 1991.

The first analyses that were made of data from the BHPS confirmed the overwhelming importance of work. Between 1991 and 1995, for example, almost 80 per cent of those who moved from worklessness to work had escaped from the bottom fifth of the income distribution as a result. Put the other way round, nearly 66 per cent of those who left the bottom fifth did so because someone in the household either got a job or increased his or her earnings (Jenkins 1999). It is statistics such as these that have fuelled New Labour's drive to 'embed work as the cornerstone of the welfare system for all those of working age' (Blair 2001: 3).

New Labour has sought to achieve this objective in two ways: first, by encouraging – or in some cases compelling – people to move from welfare to paid employment; second, by boosting the incomes of those who do so through a series of tax credits. The merits of this approach have been extensively discussed. Space does not permit a full account of these discussions, but there are four issues that should be mentioned briefly: the use of compulsion, the position of lone parents, the role of in-work benefits and the overall impact of the New Deal programmes.

There are now six New Deals, of which the largest and most important is that targeted at young people, defined as those aged between 18 and 24. The most striking feature of this New Deal for Young People (NDYP) is that it is compulsory. In announcing Labour's original proposals in November 1995, Gordon Brown, then Shadow Chancellor, stated that 'simply remaining unemployed and permanently on benefit' would no longer be condoned (King and Wickham-Jones 1999: 258). A young person who had been on benefit for six months would be required to take one of four options: full-time education, a job in the private sector subsidized by a tax rebate of £60 a week, work with a voluntary agency or a placement on an Environmental Task Force. Those who refused would face benefit sanctions. This message has since become so familiar that it is hard to appreciate how radical it was in 1995. The introduction of compulsion represented a massive U-turn for the Labour Party, and one that was opposed by senior members of the Shadow Cabinet and by many of those who would be required to implement the programme.

Subsequent New Deal programmes have been targeted at lone parents, disabled people and the partners of the unemployed. These programmes are broadly voluntary, but in 1999 the Employment Service began to pilot a new programme entitled ONE. This provides a single entry point to both the employment service and the benefits system for all claimants, and from April 2000 it became mandatory for all claimants in the pilot areas to attend an initial 'work-focused' interview with a personal advisor. Even this very limited measure of compulsion, however, has proved controversial, especially in relation to lone parents. It has, for example, been criticized by Duncan and Edwards (1999) on the grounds that the decision whether or not to combine work and motherhood is a socially and culturally situated moral choice, not a matter of rational economic calculation. At the same time social conservatives have argued that the imposition of work requirements upon lone mothers is against the interests of their children (Phillips 1997a, b). It was seen in Chapter 6 that welfare policy in the USA rests on the unequivocal assumption that all lone parents will look for paid employment, and this represents a central difference between the policy debates in the two countries (Deacon 2000, 2001).

There has been no such constraint, however, upon the introduction in Britain of US-style measures to 'make work pay'. The introduction of the Working Families Tax Credit has been followed in short order by the announcement of a Childcare Tax Credit and a Child Tax Credit (HM Treasury 2000). The design of these benefits is horrendously complex, but their role in welfare reform is mercifully simple. As in the USA, they are intended not just to create incentives to work, but to prevent an injustice. They reflect a belief that if work is to be enforced, then it must be rewarded. As Tony Blair put it in a speech in 1997, 'work must be made to pay if welfare is to be made to work' (Blair 1997: 6).

It is, of course, too early to form a definitive judgement on whether or not New Labour really has 'made welfare work'. As with PRWORA in the USA, the British New Deal has been implemented in an exceptionally benign economic climate. As in the USA again the key question is how far welfare reform has contributed to that economic climate and how far it has simply benefited from it. What is not in dispute is that by the time of the election in 2001 unemployment had fallen below a million for the first time since 1975, long-term unemployment was lower than at any time since 1979 and over 280,000 young people had left the New Deal for jobs (DfEE 2001). Perhaps the most authoritative assessment to date of the New Deals is that made by Jane Millar. She concludes that their impact has been positive, and that the introduction of personal advisors to provide claimants with counselling and encouragement has been a success. She adds, however, that the New Deals have been most effective for those most job-ready, and that they will have to work harder in order to reach those with multiple disadvantages and special needs (Millar 2000: viii).

It should not be forgotten that the previous Conservative government had introduced a range of measures to increase the pressure upon unemployed claimants to accept the jobs that were available. The difference between the two is that New Labour has widened the scope of these programmes. It has begun to shift the boundary between those who are expected to look to the labour market and those who are not. David Price, a former senior official in the Employment Agency, has provided a balanced assessment of the extent to which the New Deal programmes represent a departure from the approach of the Conservatives.

> The philosophy of 'welfare to work' which underlies these programmes is broadly consistent with the approach of Conservative governments over the previous ten years, but the concept of welfare has been broadened from the claimant unemployed to include groups such as single parents and those on incapacity benefit.
>
> (Price 2000: 311)

What is most important here is not the detail of how New Labour has broadened the concept of welfare to work in this way, but why it has sought to do so. The critical point is that its focus upon work and its rhetoric about the obligations of claimants are two sides of the same coin. Taken together they should be seen as an attempt to restructure welfare in ways that minimize the value conflicts discussed in Chapter 5 and so provide a basis for rebuilding popular support for welfare.

Rebuilding popular support for welfare

Both in opposition and in government New Labour has been preoccupied with the need to rebuild popular support for welfare. It has tried to do this in part through a public acknowledgement of the need to 'modernize' welfare. In 1998, for example, Tony Blair declared that the present welfare state was no more tailored to people's needs than a car or television set designed 50 years ago (Blair 1998b). The main thrust of his appeal, however, has been to what he calls the 'enlightened self-interest' of the electorate. In a speech in South Africa in 1996 he argued that the freedom of individuals to pursue their own interests had to be 'tempered by the recognition of a common interest which must take precedence over particular interests'.

> This is not a denial of self interest. This isn't a killjoy philosophy. This is enlightened self interest. In a society in which opportunity is extended we have greater security, our streets are safer, our young people more motivated, our ambitions better fulfilled.
>
> (Blair 1996: 9)

This notion of enlightened self-interest provides a rationale for the use of compulsion within welfare to work and other programmes and also forms the basis of New Labour's appeal to the wider electorate. On the one hand, welfare is to be used to encourage, cajole and compel people to act in ways which may be unattractive in the short run but can be expected to enhance their prospects in the longer term. On the other hand, the public is to be persuaded that the money spent on welfare is not being wasted, and that the recipients are meeting their obligations. Among other things this has led ministers to adopt an aggressive stance towards the deterrence and detection of benefit fraud.

This stance is in part a response to new evidence on the extent of fraud and abuse and the consequent scope for expenditure savings (DSS 1999b, 2000). Nevertheless, the main reason why New Labour has been so anxious to publicize its campaign against fraud is its belief that public support for welfare is eroded by the failure to stop people defrauding the benefit system (DSS 1998b: iii). It was seen in Chapter 2 that Frank Field had always argued that the public would 'stump up' the money for welfare 'only if they approve of the behaviour of those for whom they are contributing' (Field 1997: 24–5). The same point was made rather more tactfully by Tony Blair in his speech in South Africa: 'I think that matching opportunity and responsibility is the only way in the modern world to obtain consent from the public to fund the welfare state. It has to become the new deal for 21st century welfare' (Blair 1996: 10).

Blair, however, was also at pains to emphasize that this 'new deal' had to be 'something deeper than merely a contractual relationship' between government and voters. A 'decent society' had to be 'founded on duty'. It required that people accept 'a significant degree of responsibility' for others. Enlisting popular support for welfare, then, was not simply an end in itself. It was an essential first step if those collective responsibilities were to be recognized and met. In the Beveridge Lecture of March 1999, Blair returned to the 'great challenge' of how to 'make the welfare state popular again'. It was also in this lecture that he declared that it was the 'historic aim' of his government 'for ours to be the first generation to end child poverty' (Blair 1999: 17).

Ending child poverty as we know it

Tony Blair's announcement of a poverty target marked a significant change in New Labour rhetoric. Both in opposition and in the early days in government Blair and his senior colleagues had spoken little about poverty. They had chosen instead to employ the language of the dependency theorists discussed in earlier chapters. Blair himself had insisted that 'our collective duty as a society' was first and foremost 'to tackle the growing underclass' which was 'cut off from society's mainstream' (Blair 1996: 9). Peter Mandelson, one of the prime architects of New Labour, had spoken of 'today's and tomorrow's underclass', which consisted of 'people who have lost hope' and are 'trapped in fatalism'. The 'people we are concerned about', he added, 'will not have their long-term problems addressed by an extra pound a week on their benefits' (Mandelson 1997: 6–7).

On other occasions ministers did talk about processes of social exclusion, by which they meant the mutually reinforcing effects of low incomes, poor health, inadequate housing and discrimination on the grounds of race and gender (Levitas 1998). Very rarely, however, did they focus specifically upon low incomes, and hardly ever did they use what came to be known as the 'p-word'. Not, that is, until Blair so dramatically committed them to eliminate child poverty in 20 years.

It is far from clear what prompted this change of emphasis. One factor, however, was the growing recognition of the extent to which the opportunities open to people during their lifetime are diminished by the experience of poverty in childhood. In the words of a government document,

> The key to tackling disadvantage in the future is the eradication of child poverty. Children who grow up in disadvantaged families generally do less well at school, and are more likely to suffer unemployment, low pay and poor health in adulthood. This poverty of opportunity is then more likely to be experienced by the next generation of children.
>
> (DSS 1999a: 5)

The important point here is that ending child poverty came to be seen and presented less as an objective in itself and more as a first step towards the broader aim of reducing inequalities of opportunity. Social exclusion came to be seen as exclusion from opportunities, and child poverty came to be seen as a root cause of that exclusion.

In some respects there is nothing very remarkable about this. It was seen in Chapter 1 that the pursuit of equality had long been the central objective of labour politics. Similarly, Anthony Giddens has argued that what distinguishes the third way from Thatcherism is its concern with equality and redistribution (Giddens 2000: 89). What is more surprising perhaps is that it was the Chancellor of the Exchequer – Gordon Brown – who played the central role in bringing child poverty to the top of New Labour's welfare agenda.

Just before the 1997 election Brown had argued that an incoming Labour government must retain the party's traditional commitment to equality. He had done so, moreover, in the language of Christian socialism. The starting point, he said, must be 'a fundamental belief in the equal worth of every human being'. This meant that all must have 'an equal chance' to 'develop the potential with which they were born' (Brown 1999: 40). In order to fulfil their potential, individuals require opportunities to work, to learn and train and to exercise some control over the decisions that affect their lives. Moreover, the denial of such opportunities is not only an affront to social justice but is also an obstacle to economic management. What is right on 'ethical grounds' is 'good for the economy too'. 'Today, in an economy where skills are the essential means of production, the denial of opportunity has become an unacceptable inefficiency, a barrier to prosperity' (p. 41).

A Labour government, Brown argued, should take a 'demanding view of equality of opportunity' and work 'to prevent the permanent entrenchment of privilege from whatever source it came' (p. 43). It was against this background that in March 1999 the Treasury published what it described in a press release as 'shocking conclusions' about the 'passage of inequality from generation to generation' and about the 'persistent and scarring nature' of childhood poverty. These conclusions were drawn largely from analyses of panel data that had been presented at a workshop organized by the Treasury in the previous November. The central message was that 'people's life chances are determined by who their parents were rather than their own talents and efforts' (HM Treasury 1999: 31). 'Childhood disadvantage frequently leads to low educational attainment, low educational attainment leads to low pay and low employment, which in turn leads to low income and denial of opportunity for the next generation' (p. 27).

The key 'transmission mechanism' was education. Studies of the educational development of children born in 1970 showed that those from privileged backgrounds were markedly ahead at the age of 22 months, and that the differential between them and children from poor backgrounds continued to widen thereafter (p. 29). This was not the whole story, however, since statistical research showed that poverty 'has a further, distinct effect, over and above its impact on education' (p. 33). All of this was further compounded in the most deprived areas, in which 'whole communities find themselves trapped outside mainstream society' by high rates of worklessness and crime, poor health and low educational achievement (DSS 1999a: 138).

New Labour has sought to break the 'cycle of decline' that threatens such communities by expanding work opportunities and by introducing a cluster of new agencies and initiatives to promote community development. At the same time it has made significant increases to the level of benefits paid in respect of children. By April 2000, for example, the level of income support benefits for children under 11 had risen by 72 per cent in real terms since New Labour took office, and that of child benefit by 26 per cent (HM Treasury 2000: 10). The latter increase is particularly noteworthy since it is a rare example of a rise in universal rather than means-tested benefits.

Retaining the means test

There is one striking omission from New Labour's welfare agenda. The Green Paper and subsequent policy documents have talked again and again about the need for an active benefits system, but they have said virtually nothing about the problem of means testing.

It was seen in Chapter 2 that when in opposition Frank Field had developed a powerful critique of means-tested benefits. He had argued that they penalized the very behaviours that welfare should promote, and thereby corroded the characters of those who claimed them. Moreover, Field's call for an expansion of contributory insurance had been echoed by others who did not share his preoccupation with personal character. The Borrie Commission, for example, also emphasized the ways in which means tests punished those who raised their earnings or built up savings. It too believed that a 'new social insurance scheme should be the foundation of long term reform' (Borrie Commission 1994: 227).

These arguments, however, were not made in the Green Paper, which Field presented to Parliament as Minister for Welfare Reform in March 1998. Their absence was all the more striking because a recurring theme of the Green Paper was that changing the benefits system would change behaviour. A more active administration would stimulate and cajole people into doing more to find a job. The new tax credits would encourage them to work harder and longer. A better designed system would deter fraud. Nowhere in the Green Paper, however, was this logic applied to means testing.

It was widely known that the publication of the Green Paper had been delayed by conflicts between the DSS and the Treasury and, within the DSS itself, between Field and the Secretary of State, Harriet Harman. The critical issue had been the cost of Field's proposed stakeholder welfare. It was seen in Chapter 2 that Field had to confront the problem of how to persuade an electorate motivated by self-interest to support a substantial measure of redistribution. The voters had to be convinced that it was in their self-interest to pay not just for themselves but for carers and others whom Field wished to include. Stakeholder welfare was an ingenious attempt to square this circle, but the Green Paper suggested that Field had not convinced his colleagues that it was politically viable. The higher contributions that would have been required would have jeopardized the broader aim of rebuilding popular support for welfare, while the essential optimism of that project was not compatible with Field's focus upon the imperfections of human nature (Deacon 1998).

This appeared to be confirmed when Field was effectively sacked in July 1998, and policy has since moved decisively against any expansion of social insurance. A form of stakeholder pension has been introduced, but this bears little relation to Field's original proposals. Moreover, both the new Minimum Income Guarantee for pensioners and the new tax credits for working families represent a significant expansion of means-tested provision. The Conservative MP David Willets has argued that they will inevitably erode incentives to work and save in language similar to that of Field himself.

> There is a sort of bleak, telescopic philanthropy about the Brown agenda. If focuses on tapers, means tests, and computer modelling of finely calculated effects on household incomes. There is little recognition of the values and institutions which help flesh and blood families through bad times as well as good.
>
> (Willets 2000: 27)

In reality the means test has become more and more a necessary evil, its defects glossed over in ministers' speeches and official documents. Two things have driven New Labour closer to targeting. First, it is trying to combat social exclusion while trimming the welfare budget in order to release more resources for education and the NHS. Second, it has remained fearful of the electoral consequences of too explicit a commitment to redistribution, and gave a commitment during the general election of 2001 that it would not raise income tax rates. In the words of the Prime Minister's advisor on education, Andrew Adonis, 'while New Labour wants to help the poor as a matter of principle, it refuses to hit the rich as a matter of principle'. It is this, Adonis adds, 'which separates Old Left from New Left' (quoted in Page 2000: 619). It is also this that reinforces the trend towards targeted benefits, which seem to provide a mechanism for helping the poor at minimum cost to everyone else.

Conclusion

It will be apparent that New Labour's approach to welfare reform draws upon each of the perspectives outlined in this book. Indeed, it was argued at the beginning of the chapter that the elusive third way is best understood as an attempt to achieve a new accommodation between particular elements of these perspectives. Before discussing this further, however, it is perhaps worth emphasizing for one final time that nothing in this book is intended to suggest that these ideas are the only reason why centre left thinking on welfare has changed so radically in recent years. On the contrary, New Labour's rethink on welfare was only one facet of the wholesale transformation of the party that followed the election of Tony Blair as leader in 1994. That transformation was itself a response to a number of factors, but by far the most important were the experience of four successive election defeats and the change in the perception of what the electorate was prepared to pay for.

That said, it is clear that the most important intellectual influence upon New Labour's approach to welfare reform is that of communitarianism. In Driver and Martell's (1998: 29) words, communitaranism lies 'at the heart' of New Labour politics. It is the communitarian critique of libertarianism that provides the basis of New Labour's attack on Thatcherism, and it is communitarianism's emphasis upon obligations and duties that most sharply distinguishes New Labour from Old Labour. In the case of welfare reform, however, that emphasis upon the obligations of welfare claimants has found expression in welfare-to-work programmes that have been shaped by the notions of welfare as transitional assistance that were discussed in Chapter 5. In many respects Labour's New Deals are closer to David Ellwood's original ideas than was the legislation eventually passed in the USA (Deacon 2000: 13). Indeed, Howard Glennerster has observed that the Blair government had implemented all of the main recommendations in *Poor Support* within two years of taking office (Glennerster 2000a: 17).

At the same time, it must be acknowledged that neither of these two influences can be understood in isolation. The welfare-to-work programmes also reflected European and Australian thinking and experiences. Similarly, the impact of modern communitarianism upon New Labour has been all the greater because of its obvious resonance with the older traditions of English Christian socialism, and especially with Tawney's arguments about the need for right social relationships and a common culture. It is the combination of these that has been so influential, a combination that is best understood as 'Anglicanized communitarianism' (Deacon 2000: 11). In the midst of the general election campaign of 2001 Tony Blair was still quoting Tawney on the dangers of divorcing rights and responsibilities (Blair 2001: 2).

Blair did not, however, quote Titmuss, and New Labour's evident lack of faith in the altruism of the electorate has caused dismay among some commentators on the left. Robert Page, for example, argues that its 'reluctance to maintain altruistic goals amounts to nothing less than a seismic break' from Labour's past, because the party is no longer 'attempting to create a more equal society in which the ideal of caring for strangers is seen as the ultimate objective' (Page 2000: 7). It is a matter of interpretation, however, how far this is a difference of ends or of means. It has been shown that although New Labour may have had little to say about caring for strangers, it has had much to say about child poverty and equality of opportunity. Indeed, it is on this issue that New Labour's approach differs most sharply from that of the New Democrats in the USA.

New Labour's commitment to end child poverty is likely to remain a central issue in its second term in government. It is interesting, therefore, to examine New Labour's interpretation of the data on poverty and the transmission of deprivation in the light of the perspectives discussed in this book. There is no doubt that New Labour's understanding of the causes of poverty is primarily a structural one. It does not deny that behaviours and attitudes help to explain why some people are unemployed for long periods, or why poverty affects successive generations of the same family. In essence, however, those behaviours are seen as a consequence rather than a cause of social deprivation. It shares William Julius Wilson's belief that if public policy succeeds in improving the economic prospects of such communities, then those behaviours, 'no longer sustained and nourished by persistent joblessness, will gradually fade' (Wilson 1997: 238). This analysis is expressed with particular clarity in the report of the Policy Action Team on Jobs, one of a number of such teams set up to review policy in respect of the poorest neighbourhoods.

> The very dynamism of the economy acts to create new pockets of deprivation as long-established industries give way to new ones, in new locations, demanding new skills. These pockets persist because of structural barriers that prevent markets working to get rid of poor areas: poor school and training standards mean that young people do not acquire the skills they need to compete effectively for many of the jobs being generated; lack of amenity and crime mean that many people who get jobs and prosper move out; poor physical and human capital deters inward investment.
>
> (DfEE 2000: 1)

Similarly, the Treasury report on transmitted deprivation was quick to point out that the slower educational development of poor children cannot be ascribed to poor parenting in problem families, but is linked to a 'series of factors that are more likely to occur in disadvantaged families'. These include large family size, poor and overcrowded housing, low birth weight and unemployment of the father. It follows that the most effective interventions are those that are 'non-stigmatizing' and 'avoid labelling problem families' (HM Treasury 1999: 29–30). Elsewhere New Labour's first 'poverty report' acknowledges that 'not all children born into low income families fare badly in later life' and that 'parental attitudes and interest in education have a significant effect on educational attainment'. It goes on, however, to argue that governments cannot expect to stimulate a higher level of parental interest without first tackling the broader and more deep rooted 'poverty of ambition' which characterizes such communities. This in turn will require the provision of more effective schools and far greater opportunities for employment (DSS 1999a: 44–5).

At the same time, New Labour expects that those who are currently experiencing exclusion will take advantage of the opportunities that it will create, and is willing to compel them to do so if necessary. It believes that the growth of poverty in the past is explained at least in part by the failure of previous governments to provide the requisite encouragement and pressure. A government document, for example, argues that the 'passive administration of Invalidity Benefit is likely to have exacerbated' the increase in inactivity amongst older men. This is because its 'more generous level encouraged people to define themselves as incapacitated rather than unemployed', and because there was 'inadequate scrutiny of claims to benefits' (DSS 2000: 37). There are clear echoes here of Lawrence Mead's understanding of a culture of poverty as one that condones the failure of the poor to meet their obligations and to conform to agreed social norms.

What is most significant for this book, however, is the way in which New Labour has integrated different perspectives. It views social exclusion as both structural – because people are excluded by deprivations that are transmitted across generations – and individual – because if people do not take advantage of their opportunities they will have excluded themselves. In policy terms this produces a package of measures, some of which are designed to level the playing field and some of which are designed to activate the players.

Further reading

The best single account of the politics of New Labour is that by Driver and Martell (1998). A powerful critique of the intellectual influences upon New Labour is to be found in Levitas (1998), while the essays in Powell (1999) and Novak (1998) provide a comprehensive discussion of New Labour's third way on welfare. Perhaps the most trenchant, and certainly the most witty, criticisms of the idea of a third way are those made by Klein and Rafferty (1999). There are also a number of essays on the third way and New Labour's approach to welfare in various volumes of the *Social Policy Review* (May *et al.* 1997; Brundson *et al.* 1998; Dean and Woods 1999). The background to New Labour's commitment to abolish child poverty is discussed in Walker (1999) and Fimister (2001), and an authoritative assessment of the progress made by January 2000 is given in Piachaud and Sutherland (2001). The implementation of the New Deals is monitored in *Working Brief*, published by the Unemployment Unit and Youthaid, and on various official websites that can be accessed through www.newdeal.gov.uk. The continual reorganization of government departments means that websites quickly become out of date. The safest course is usually to begin at the somewhat ironically titled www.open.gov.uk.

Conclusion

This book has examined a number of different perspectives on welfare. Each of these perspectives has put forward a distinctive view of what should be the objectives of welfare, and how those objectives could be achieved. These views are in turn grounded in contrasting assumptions about human nature. The writers whose work was examined in previous chapters all began with the premise that, in James Q. Wilson's words, human beings possess 'a set of traits and predispositions that limits what we may do and suggests guides to what we must do' (Wilson 1995: 206). Nevertheless, they have very different views of what these 'traits and predispositions' are, and of the ways in which they constrain and guide welfare policy.

The book has sought to justify its focus upon welfare perspectives on two grounds. First, it has shown how policy debates in Britain and the United States have drawn upon elements of the perspectives that have been outlined, and how the welfare reforms implemented in both countries have been shaped by those debates. Second, it has argued, and I hope has demonstrated, that the debates between these perspectives are of compelling interest to students of welfare and of public policy in general.

The approach that is taken in this concluding chapter is different from that adopted in the rest of the book. Hitherto the emphasis has been upon exposition and explanation. The intention has been to set out the assumptions and arguments of each perspective and to explain why they take the form that they do. The purpose of this chapter is to provide a framework within which the reader can begin to form his or her own judgement about the persuasiveness of the perspectives and the validity of their assumptions. It does this by using quotations from the commentators discussed earlier to illustrate the answers they would give to a series of questions about human nature and about the motivation and capacities of poor people. A flow chart is drawn on the basis of these answers in order to show how the views that the commentators take of the claims and obligations of the poor are reflected in their approach to welfare reform.

It must be acknowledged that this is something of an artificial exercise. It is artificial in the sense that the quotations that are used exaggerate, even caricature, the differences between the perspectives. This is done deliberately in order to illustrate as sharply as possible the choices that have to be made and thereby to stimulate argument and debate. Even so, it is still necessary to begin with a brief explanation of the ways in which the perspectives have been categorized and the questions framed.

A typology of the perspectives

It has been stressed throughout the book that there are significant areas of overlap between the perspectives that it has identified. Paternalism and communitarianism, for example, both emphasize the obligations of citizenship but seek to enforce them in different ways. Similarly, the paternalism of Lawrence Mead and the libertarian conservatism of Charles Murray both focus upon the attitudes and values of the poor, but have different views of the role that government should play in changing those attitudes and values. Conversely, Titmuss and the communitarians both believe that welfare can help to foster a sense of community, but whereas Titmuss talks primarily about the needs and entitlements of the members of those communities, communitarians talk primarily about their responsibilities and obligations.

It follows that it would be possible to produce a number of different typologies of the perspectives, each of which would represent a different balance of the same core elements. There is, however, one typology that is especially helpful in classifying the perspectives. This is Stuart White's (1998) analysis of the contributions to the third way debate. White argues that what he calls 'third way thinking' is characterized by a dual commitment to the values of 'real opportunity' and 'civic responsibility'. By a commitment to 'real opportunity' he means an acceptance that everyone should have access to a minimally decent share of such basic goods as education, income and jobs. By a commitment to 'civic responsibility' he means an acceptance that individuals should not displace on to others the costs of their lifestyle choices: that they should recognize their responsibilities to nurture their children, to pay a fair level of taxation and to protect the natural environment (White 1998: 19). It is the importance placed upon these two values that distinguishes proponents of a third way from both the old left – which had little to say about 'civic responsibility' – and the new right – which had even less to say about 'real opportunity'.

White goes on to argue, however, that while participants in the third way debate agree on the importance of these values, they nevertheless 'disagree over their interpretation'. In particular he identifies 'two important lines of division amongst those who subscribe to the broad framework of third way thinking'. The first division is between 'leftists' and 'centrists' over the degree of redistribution that is needed to create real opportunity. The second division is between liberals and communitarians over the range of behaviours that the state should seek to regulate and the obligations it is entitled to enforce (p. 25).

It is these two 'lines of division' that provide a basis for classifying the perspectives discussed in this book (Figure 9.1). It is clear, for example, that the quasi-Titmuss paradigm is a liberal/leftist position in White's terms, since it argues that real opportunity requires a substantial measure of redistribution but that the state should play a very limited role in the regulation of behaviour. It is equally clear that paternalism is the exact opposite – centrist and communitarian. Similarly, Charles Murray is close to the liberal/centrist position. It is also a relatively straightforward matter to locate the approach of New Labour and of the New Democrats. Both would be near to the middle of both continua, but with New Labour more leftist and the New Democrats more paternalist.

Other perspectives, however, do not 'fit' so well. White's communitarian–liberal continuum, for example, does not distinguish between those who look to the state to enforce obligations and those who look to more informal communal pressures. A more serious problem, however, is that White's typology does not reflect the different assumptions that are made about the capacities of poor people. Frank Field, for example, is close to what White would term a leftist/communitarian position in that he advocates both

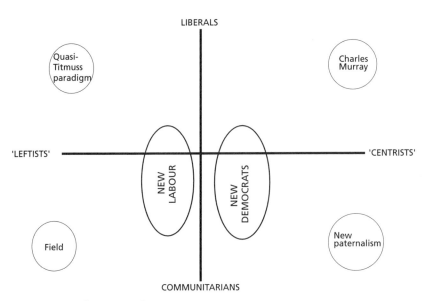

Figure 9.1 White's typology

redistribution and conditionality. This places him in the opposite quadrant to Charles Murray, although it was seen in Chapter 2 that both Field and Murray assume that the overwhelming majority of the poor are rational actors and both reject the argument of the new paternalists that the long-term poor are dysfunctional or incompetent. For the purposes of this chapter, then, White's typology needs to be supplemented by a more focused approach that addresses directly the relationship between arguments about human nature and debates about welfare.

From human nature to welfare reform: the 'flow chart'

None of the commentators discussed in this book is poor, or at least they were not poor when they produced the works discussed here. They all, however, put forward a view about the claims that poor people are entitled to make upon the wider community and what obligations they have towards the wider community in return. These views are laid out in the 'flow chart' in Figure 9.2, and explored below, beginning with the question of whether welfare policy should be primarily concerned with social inequalities or with personal behaviour.

Question 1: Is it the task of welfare to change the attitudes and behaviour of claimants?

One unequivocal answer to this question is provided in *Quote 1A*. This is taken from Michael Harrington's book *The Other America*, which was first published forty years ago. It is a long quotation, but it repays study since it is still the most eloquent and most powerful statement of the argument that the job of welfare is not to concern itself with the behaviour of those who experience poverty but to tackle the structural causes of that poverty.

Quote 1A: 'No'

Michael Harrington: The structural causes of poverty

There are, one must assume, citizens of the other America who choose impoverishment out of fear of work (though, writing it down, I really do not believe it). But the real explanation of why the poor are where they are is that they made the mistake of being born to the wrong parents, in the wrong section of the country, in the wrong industry, or in the wrong racial or ethnic group. Once that mistake has been made, they could have been paragons of will and morality, but most of them would never even have had a chance to get out of the other America.

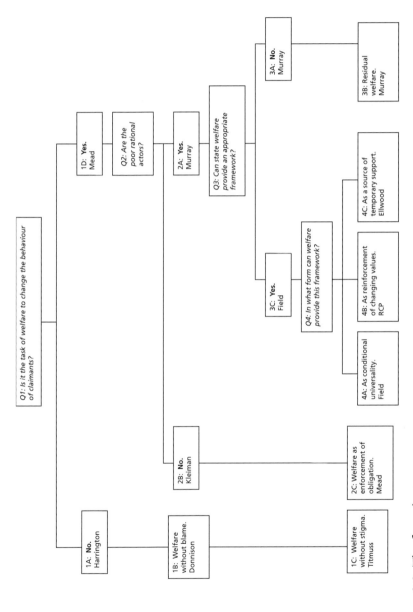

Figure 9.2 The flow chart

In a sense, one might define the contemporary poor in the United States as those who, for reasons beyond their control, cannot help themselves. All the most decisive factors making for opportunity and advance are against them. They are born going downward, and most of them stay down.

Here is one of the most familiar forms of the vicious circle of poverty. The poor get sick more than anyone else in the society. That is because they live in slums, jammed together under unhygienic conditions; they have inadequate diets, and cannot get decent medical care. When they become sick, they are sick longer than any other group in the society. Because they are sick more often and longer than anyone else, they lose wages and work, and find it difficult to hold a steady job. And because of this, they cannot pay for good housing, for a nutritious diet, for doctors.

The individual cannot usually break out of this vicious circle. Neither can the group, for it lacks the social energy and political strength to turn its misery into a cause. Only the larger society, with its help and resources, can really make it possible for these people to help themselves. Yet those who could make the difference too often refuse to act because of their ignorant smug moralisms. They view the effects of poverty – above all the warping of the will and spirits that is a consequence of being poor – as choices. Understanding the vicious circle is an important step in breaking down this prejudice.

The other Americans are those who live at a level of life beneath moral choice, who are so submerged in their poverty that one cannot begin to talk about free choice. The point is not to make them wards of the state. Rather, society must help them before they can help themselves.

(Harrington 1997: 14–16, 162)

Harrington's anger at the 'ignorant smug moralisms' of those who blamed the poor for their own poverty was fuelled by the blatant injustices of American society in the 1950s. He believed that it was patently obvious to anyone who cared to look that the poor were victims of inequality, trapped in 'the other America' by forces beyond the control of any individual. That anger continues to be expressed in present-day Britain by commentators committed to what has been termed in this book the quasi-Titmuss paradigm. It was seen in Chapter 1 that these commentators point to the persistence of inequalities in income, wealth and health, and to the disproportionate impact of those inequalities upon women and members of ethnic minorities (Shaw *et al.* 1999; Pantazis and Gordon 2000). The poor, they argue, did not and still do not need governments to provide them with advice, counselling or instruction about how to live their lives. What they do need is a fairer share of resources and the same opportunities as everyone else.

One implication of this is that commentators must be prepared to challenge attempts to distinguish between the deserving and the non-deserving poor, and to scapegoat some of the poor as a feckless underclass. In *Quote 1B* David Donnison argues that such views became the 'conventional wisdom' in Britain in the 1980s because they were formulated by and served to reassure 'dominant groups' in society.

More broadly, the argument is that if welfare is to succeed in reducing inequalities then it has to accept what Richard Titmuss calls in *Quote 1C* the fundamental challenge of redistributing resources without stigma. The two quotations cited here are taken from lectures he gave in 1966 and 1967. In them he sets out the central case for non-judgemental welfare: that it must be viewed as a form of compensation to those who bear a disproportionate share of the social costs of economic and technological advance. Seen in this light, welfare is something that is 'owed' to the poor, it is their entitlement and so must be provided without conditions regarding personal circumstances or behaviour.

Quote 1B: 'No'

David Donnison: Welfare without blame

The dominant groups in any society formulate the political drama which informs the thinking of their day and defines its heroes and heroines, its villains, its social problems and its public morality. This is the 'conventional wisdom' of their times. It imposes upon the victims of the problems it identifies – on the people most likely to suffer from these difficulties – much of the blame for them. The conventional wisdom teaches that it is the behaviour of the victims which must be changed if these problems are to be solved. That view of the world reassures the dominant groups. It has to be challenged before the victims can extend their own rights.

(Donnison 1991: 71)

Quote 1C: 'No'

Richard Titmuss: Welfare without stigma

The emphasis today on 'welfare' and the 'benefits of welfare' often tends to obscure the fundamental fact that for many consumers the services used are not essentially benefits or increments to welfare at all: they represent partial compensations for disservices, for social costs and social insecurities which are the product of a rapidly changing industrial–urban society. They are part of the price we pay to some people for bearing some of the costs of other people's progress: the obsolescence of skills, redundancies, premature retirements, accidents, many categories of disease and handicap, urban blight and slum clearance, smoke pollution and a hundred-and-one other socially generated disservices. They are the socially caused diswelfares; the losses involved in aggregate welfare gains.

The essential issue here is . . . how to channel proportionately more economic and social resources to the poor, the handicapped, the educationally deprived and other minority groups. We cannot now, just because we are getting richer, disengage ourselves from the fundamental challenge of distributing social rights without stigma.

(Titmuss 1968: 133, 143)

It is difficult to imagine a greater contrast of views than that between David Donnison and the author of the next quotation, Lawrence Mead. *Quote 1D* is taken from Mead's *The New Politics of Poverty* (1992). It was seen in Chapter 3 that Mead argues that the politics of conduct have now supplanted the politics of class. The long-term poor are trapped not by the structural inequalities that Harrington described, but by their own failure to work and to accept responsibility for themselves and their dependants. Until very recently this failure was condoned by policy-making elites that were overly influenced by the arguments of Harrington and others. Far from scapegoating the poor, the 'conventional wisdom' was long dominated by the 'exceptive liberalism' that he parodies in the passage quoted here.

Quote 1D: 'Yes'

Lawrence Mead: Welfare without passivity

This diffuse, determinist style of analysis, which I have termed sociologism, construes the personality as essentially passive: The poor are seen as inert, not active. They are spoken of in the passive voice. They are people who are or have been disadvantaged in multiple ways. They do not do things but rather have things done to them. They are the objects, not the subjects of action. They are not to blame for conditions such as dropping out of school, AIDS, or drug addiction, but rather 'at risk' from them. They 'experience' behaviors such as crime or illegitimacy rather than commit them.

(Mead 1992: 129–30)

Question 2: Are the poor rational actors, able to identify and pursue their own self-interest?

The second question is addressed to those who believe that welfare should try to change behaviour. It is a question that receives a very different answer from those who see the role of welfare as to channel the pursuit of self-interest and from those who see its role as to exercise authority over the lives of the poor. *Quote 2A* is taken from Charles Murray's *Losing Ground*. It sets out his core argument that the poor are no less rational than anyone else. The difference, he says, is in their circumstances. What is rational behaviour for the poor is not necessarily the same as what is rational for those who are not poor. In contrast, *Quote 2B* from Mark Kleiman sets out the central assumption of the new paternalism, that it is often necessary to force the poor to act in their own self-interest. *Quote 2C* from Lawrence Mead outlines what such paternalism involves in practice.

Quote 2A: 'Yes'

Charles Murray: The rationality of the poor

I begin with the proposition that all, poor and not-poor alike, use the same general calculus in arriving at decisions; only the exigencies are different. Poor people play with fewer chips and cannot wait as long for results. Therefore they tend to reach decisions that a more affluent person would not reach . . . [The] behaviours that are 'rational' are different at different economic levels.

(Murray 1984: 155)

Quote 2B: 'No'

Mark Kleiman: The philosophy of paternalism

All paternalist interventions rest on one primary insight: that there are large and systematic divergences between the actual behaviour of some human beings, or of human beings generally under some circumstances, and the canons of rationally self-interested action as microeconomists understand them.

(Kleiman 1997: 187)

Quote 2C: 'No'

Lawrence Mead: The enforcement of obligations

Policies that enforce must be directive. That is, they must tell the people obligated what they are supposed to do. Thus paternalism includes policies that make school attendance compulsory for children or require welfare recipients to work as a condition of receiving aid. It excludes programs that seek to influence behaviour through benefits or opportunities without telling them what to do.

(Mead 1997a: 4)

Question 3: Can state welfare provide an appropriate framework for the pursuit of self-interest?

The third question is addressed to those who believe that the majority of the poor should be regarded as rational actors. It is this question that distinguishes the perspective of Charles Murray from those of the other commentators discussed in this book. The first quotation from Murray, *Quote 3A*, is long but like that from Harrington repays careful study. In it he argues that in order to fulfil their potential people have to be free to take their own decisions but also accountable for the consequences of those decisions. State welfare in whatever form constrains that freedom and undermines that accountability. This, then, is the philosophical basis of the 'abolitionist' case that was seen in Chapter 6 to have been so influential in the USA in the early 1990s. The contrast with Richard Titmuss is obvious: whereas he would eliminate stigma from welfare, Murray would use it to reinforce personal responsibility. Just as significant, however, is the contrast with the new paternalism. As the second quotation, *Quote 3B*, makes clear, Murray believes that such interventions will always fail.

Quote 3A: 'No'

Charles Murray: Welfare, freedom and accountability

To pursue happiness is to pursue the good we seek as an end in itself, that thing which, realized, expresses itself as justified satisfaction with life as a whole. The object of government is to provide a framework within which people – all people, of all temperaments and talents – can pursue happiness.

By all the evidence that science has been able to muster, people need to be self-determining, accountable and absorbed in stretching their capacities, just as they need food and shelter. The crucial question that must decisively affect policy is whether it is possible to make people feel as if they are self-determining, accountable, and realizing their capacities when they are not.

Social programs have been designed as if it were enough to get people to 'feel as if,' designed seemingly on the assumption that there can be challenge without risks, accountability without penalties, self-determination without the assumption that every person – everyone not mentally deranged – possesses freedom of will.

No concept has been more unfashionable in social policy for the last twenty-five years than 'stigma,' and no criticism has been treated as more damning than to say that such and such a policy 'stigmatizes' people . . . Government's duty is to provide an environment in which people accept responsibility for their actions. An acceptable social policy is one that validates the individual's responsibility for the consequences of his behaviour. Or to put it another way, a social policy that induces people to believe that they are not responsible for their lives is one that inhibits the pursuit of happiness and is to that extent immoral. Can then a policy that fails to stigmatize be a moral one?

(Murray 1988: 51, 131, 296)

Quote 3B: 'No'

Charles Murray: Why paternalism will always fail

[This is] asking the government to behave like a concerned friend or relative or neighbour or church congregation, helping while at the same time holding people responsible for their behavior. Governments cannot do that. They try, and the harder they try the more totalitarian they become, but they never succeed.

(Murray 1986b: 22)

A completely different answer to Question 2 is given by Frank Field in *Quote 3C*. Like Murray, he believes that the poor are rational, but unlike Murray he believes that state welfare can create a framework of incentives and penalties that will lead people to pursue their self-interest in ways which promote their own good and that of the wider community. Moreover, it can do this while redistributing resources and reducing inequalities – an objective that is anathema to Murray.

Quote 3C: 'Yes'

Frank Field: The need to create the right framework

It is not a question of seeking the means by which the values of individuals are changed. It is rather a question of setting a legal framework where natural decent instincts guided by self interest are allowed to operate in a manner which enhances the common good . . . Set the right framework – i.e. a welfare system which accepts as its starting point that individuals wish to better themselves and their families, and allows them to do so – and the 'moral improvement' (I would prefer to describe this change as an increase in social well-being) will take place.

(Field 1997: 20)

Question 4: What form should welfare take if it is to provide this framework?

This question is addressed to those commentators who do not share either Murray's abolitionist perspective or the paternalism of Mead or Kleiman. It asks what role welfare should play if it is to lead those who receive it to act in ways which promote the common good.

In *Quote 4A* Field argues that the role of welfare is to reward those behaviours and virtues that should be encouraged – such as thrift and honesty – and penalize those which should be discouraged. It can and should do this through the rules and regulations that govern entitlement to benefits.

Quote 4A

Frank Field: Welfare has a major role as a source of rewards and punishments

One of welfare's roles is to reward and to punish. The distribution of welfare is one of the great teaching forces open to advanced societies. As Christian morality becomes unsustainable without being recharged in each generation by waves of new Christian believers, so societies must seek different ways of affirming right and wrong conduct. Welfare has such a role. But here the selection for reward or punishment is self-selection (i.e. I am willing or not willing to agree to the conditions attached to benefit).

(Field 1996: 11)

The communitarian response to Question Four is given in **Quote 4B**. In effect this assigns welfare a supporting role in the attempt to change values and instil a greater sense of responsibility to the community. It was seen in Chapter 4 that the major role is to be played by moral argument.

Quote 4B

The Responsive Communitarian Platform: Welfare has a minor role in the task of changing values

Our first and foremost purpose is to affirm the moral commitment of parents, young persons, neighbours, and citizens, to affirm the importance of the communities within which such commitments take shape and are transmitted from one generation to the next. This is not primarily a legal matter. On the contrary, when a community reaches the point at which these responsibilities are largely enforced by the powers of the state, it is in deep moral crisis. If communities are to function well, most members most of the time must discharge their responsibilities because they are committed to do so, not because they fear lawsuits, penalties or jails.

(Responsive Communitarian Platform 1988: xxxvi)

The final response is that of David Ellwood in **Quote 4C**. It was seen in Chapter 5 that he believes that cash-based welfare is inherently flawed, and that it must be subject to strict time limits. The solution lies in enabling people to move from welfare to jobs, and in making sure that work 'pays'.

Quote 4C

David Ellwood: Welfare has a role as a source of temporary support

Abolishing welfare or forcing people to work for their benefits will not help. The best hope is to understand the real causes of poverty and to address them directly. The goal ought to be to ensure that everyone who behaves responsibly will avoid poverty and welfare. The big challenges to be tackled involve supporting the working poor, resolving the dual role of single parents, helping people over temporary difficulties, and offering hope to all people that they can get a job if they are willing to work.

(Ellwood 1988: 236–7)

The flow chart concludes with the six quotations that represent the six formulations of welfare that have been at the core of this book:

- unconditional universal welfare (*Quote 1C*, discussed in Chapter 1);
- conditional universal welfare (*Quote 4A*, discussed in Chapter 2);
- paternalist welfare (*Quote 2C*, discussed in Chapter 3);
- residual welfare (*Quote 3B*, discussed in Chapter 2);
- welfare as transitional assistance (*Quote 4C*, discussed in Chapter 5);
- welfare in support of moral regeneration (*Quote 4B*, discussed in Chapter 4).

The purpose of this 'flow chart', then, has been to highlight the links between the assumptions that the different commentators have made about the motives and capacities of poor people and their prescriptions for the reform of welfare. In order to do this, it had to simplify what is in reality a very complex debate. In particular, the notion of individual agency has attracted considerable attention in recent years, and has been analysed and theorized in new and exciting ways (Deacon and Mann 1999; Williams *et al.* 1999; Hogget 2001). There is also a similarly challenging literature on the nature of citizenship (Lister 1997; Dwyer 2000), and on the ways in which principles of recognition and care provide the basis for a new conceptualization of welfare (Williams 1999). This more analytical and reflective literature is beyond the scope of this book, which has focused upon normative and prescriptive approaches.

A second qualification is that the flow chart could have begun with the question of whether or not welfare should be concerned with equality. If it had, it would have first distinguished between White's 'leftists' and 'centrists' and then gone on to distinguish further between those 'leftists' by the emphasis placed upon the right to welfare, upon conditionality and upon time limits and the transition to paid employment.

The most important qualification to make about the 'flow chart', however, is that the welfare debate is not about absolutes. It is, for example, a question not of choosing to tackle inequality or dependency, but of determining the balance between these two objectives. This, of course, is somewhat easier said than done.

Finding the balance: a personal conclusion

The central purpose of this book has been to provide an introduction to the current debate about welfare, not to contribute to that debate. That said, those who have read all or part of the book are entitled to ask which perspective or combination of perspectives is closest to that of its author. The answer is, in White's terminology, a combination of leftism and communitarianism. It is a position that retains the egalitarianism of Tawney and Titmuss, but accepts the argument of Frank Field that redistributive welfare cannot neglect questions of behaviour and the argument of David Ellwood that there are severe limits to what can be achieved through cash-based welfare. With regard to the assumptions made about human nature, it shares little of Titmuss's optimism about the capacity of human beings for altruism in public affairs, but rather more of the communitarian belief that welfare can foster and help to sustain a sense of interdependence and mutual responsibility.

The question that the author finds most difficult to resolve is whether or not policy should be based on the assumption that welfare claimants are rational actors. It was seen in Chapter 6, for example, that the numbers on welfare in the USA have fallen dramatically since the welfare reforms of 1996. It is far from clear, however, how far the decline in the caseload represents a rational response to changes in the framework of rewards and penalties or is due primarily to the impact of paternalistic 'help and hassle'. Moreover, it is on this question that the new thinking about the nature of agency has done most to undermine the simple dichotomies that underpin the flow chart. It is true, for example, that the decisions which lone parents reach about paid work are not based solely upon rational calculations of the financial costs and benefits. They also reflect complex moral reasoning and assumptions about gender roles and the nature of parenthood (Duncan and Edwards 1999; Lister 1999). The conclusion must be that in Britain at least only a very small proportion of the long-term poor are 'dysfunctional' in the ways described by Lawrence Mead.

The author's position, then, is one which:

- Takes as its starting point Tawney's principle that all enjoy equality of respect by virtue of their common relationship to their Creator, and that all have an equal claim upon the resources and opportunities they need to develop to the limits of their potential.
- Accepts that this requires a commitment to greater material equality. The present inequalities in income, wealth and health are incompatible with the principle of equality of respect, as are the cross-cutting social divisions based upon race, gender, disability and sexuality.
- Accepts also that a move towards a society in which all have an equal chance to develop requires more than redistribution and an expansion of public services. The central truth of communitarianism is that it also requires that other people fulfil their responsibilities, as parents and partners as well as claimants and taxpayers. It is in this sense that welfare has at the same time to redistribute and to foster a sense of collective responsibility and personal duty.
- Accepts, finally, that this precludes the passive non-judgementalism of the

quasi-Titmuss paradigm and requires instead the adoption of conditionality and of a more demanding and sceptical approach to the delivery of welfare.

Much of the above is similar to the agenda of New Labour, or at least to the agenda as set out by its leading advocates. It reflects a somewhat unfashionable belief in the claim that there is a third way that can draw upon seemingly conflicting approaches to welfare reform. Nevertheless, it also would argue that the implementation of such a third way must involve a greater measure of redistribution than was achieved in New Labour's first term, and a reversal of its stance on social insurance and means testing.

This is, of course, just one, partial answer to some of the questions raised in this book. Others would respond to the perspectives in different ways and give very different answers. What the book has sought to do is to show how these arguments about welfare are rooted in more fundamental disagreements about the nature of human beings and the meaning of a good society. This is a debate that is both important and compelling.

Further reading

The collection of essays edited by Lewis *et al.* (2000) is an excellent introduction to new thinking about the nature of welfare. Mann (1986) and Titterton (1992) are pioneering critiques of the neglect of agency in the literature on social policy. More recent contributions to the debate about agency include Williams *et al.* (1999), Deacon and Mann (1999) and Hogget (2001). The definitive account of feminist writing on citizenship is to be found in Lister (1997), and Williams (1999) is an important discussion of the implications for welfare of the new literature on the principles of recognition and respect. A number of papers on these topics can be found on the website of the ESRC Research Group on Care, Values and the Future of Welfare, at the University of Leeds (www.leeds.ac.uk/CAVA).

Glossary

Agency The capacity of individuals to operate independently of the *social structure*. One of the central questions in sociology has long been the extent to which human behaviour should be understood as constrained or determined by *social structure*, or as purposive and involving the exercise of choice and judgement.

Altruism Behaviour that is motivated solely by a concern for the good of others. It is distinguished from behaviour that is motivated by self-interest, or is prompted by a sense of duty or the need to honour an obligation.

Behavioural This term is used in the literature on welfare to refer to explanations of social problems that focus upon the observed behaviour of those who experience those problems. The best known example is the belief that the **cycle of deprivation** is due to the parenting practices of problem families. It follows that a behavioural explanation has much in common with an **individualist** explanation. The term behavioural, however, has a different meaning in psychology. Here it refers to the belief that it is only observable behaviour that can be studied scientifically.

Christian socialism This term was originally used to refer to nineteenth- and twentieth-century writers who condemned capitalism as incompatible with Christian teaching. More recently, however, it has come to be used to refer to commentators and politicians on the centre left whose stance on social issues – including welfare reform – is influenced by their Christian faith.

Communitarian(ism) These terms are used to refer to a diverse group of theorists and commentators, and also to a social movement. At the core of communitarianism is the belief that it is necessary to restore a sense of community within Western societies and to reaffirm the obligations and duties that individuals owe to the communities in which they live. Communitarians defend the right of communities to judge the behaviour of their members, and to insist that individuals act in ways conducive to the common good of all. This has led to fierce debates with *libertarians*.

Congress (US) The legislature of the *federal government* of the United States. It consists of two houses that have broadly equal roles in the enactment of legislation: the Senate and the House of Representatives.

Culture The broadest meaning of the term culture is 'way of life'. It refers to the systems of belief and norms of behaviour within a community, and to conventions regarding dress, manners and language. In essence, it is culture that determines what is normal within a community and what is expected from its members. It follows that a cultural explanation is one which stresses the importance of such factors. The *culture of poverty* thesis explains the persistence of poverty within communities in terms of the low expectations and limited aspirations of the poor themselves. Similarly, a *dependency culture* is one in which prolonged reliance upon state benefits is regarded as normal and in which there is little expectation that people will strive to become self-reliant.

Culture of poverty See *Culture*.

Cycles of deprivation One of a number of terms and phrases which refer to the fact that poverty and deprivation is often experienced by successive generations of the same family.

Dependency culture See *Culture*.

Dynamic analyses see *Longitudinal studies*.

Egalitarian(ism) The belief that the central objective of public policy should be to achieve a more equal society. Egalitarians seek equality of respect and recognition as well as equality in the distribution of material resources.

Great Society A wide range of social reforms that were enacted in the USA in the 1960s and 1970s. They included the *War on Poverty*, as well as the decisions of the *Supreme Court* that outlawed racial segregation in schools, and the Civil Rights Acts of 1964 and 1965 that ended legal discrimination in education, employment and voting.

Human nature The qualities and capacities that are common to all people. Two questions predominate in debates about human nature. First, what are these qualities and capacities? Are we inherently selfish and aggressive beings who have to be restrained and socialized by society, or do we have an innate capacity to behave altruistically or cooperatively? The second question is whether we are all born with these qualities and capacities – 'nature' – or acquire them in interaction with others – nurture.

Income support This term is used in the UK to refer to the *means-tested benefits* paid to people who are not in full-time work and whose incomes fall below prescribed amounts. In the case of pensioners income support is normally paid as a top-up to other benefits, but for lone parents and unemployed people it is normally their sole source of income.

Income guarantee See *Means test*.

Individualism(ist) This term is used within the literature on welfare to refer to explanations of social problems that attach greater importance to the actions and values of individuals than they do to *social structure*. An individualist explanation of unemployment, for example, would be that unemployed people are not making sufficient effort to find work or to make themselves attractive to employers. In welfare, then, an individualist account has much in common with a *behavioural* account. Individualism, however, has a further, much broader meaning. It also refers to philosophical and economic doctrines that give priority to the rights and interests of individuals rather than to the rights and interests of collectivities. In this broader sense individualism is close to *libertarianism* and is opposed to *communitarianism*.

Liberal In the US literature on welfare the term liberal customarily refers to those who support higher government spending on welfare and allied programmes and who reject the notion of a *dependency culture*.

Libertarian(ism) The belief that the central objective of public policy should be to enhance the freedom and autonomy of individuals. Libertarians define freedom as the absence of restraint, and especially the absence of restraint by the state. Applied consistently, libertarianism requires that governments play a minimal role in all spheres of economic, political and social life. It thus cuts across the traditional left–right political divide. Conservative libertarians support the deregulation of capital and labour markets, and the restriction of state welfare to a minimal, residual role. Left libertarians are at the forefront of campaigns to extend civil liberties and to strengthen freedoms of expression and sexual behaviour.

Longitudinal studies Studies that re-interview the same respondents at regular intervals and so make it possible to observe the changes experienced by individuals or households over time. The data from longitudinal or *panel studies* provide the basis of *dynamic analyses* of poverty. These analyses attempt to identify the length of time households are in poverty, the extent to which they move in and out of poverty over time and the events that 'trigger' a spell in poverty.

Means test A *means-tested benefit* or service is one that is available only to individuals or households whose income and resources fall below a prescribed amount. In most cases the amount of benefit or service that claimants are entitled to receive declines progressively as their resources increase. The procedures and processes of *means testing* vary greatly and the *tax credits* discussed in the text are effectively means tests by another name. Some of these new benefits, however, are paid at a more generous rate and are presented as providing an *income guarantee* for designated groups such as low paid workers or pensioners. Once the claimant's income exceeds the guaranteed amount, the *tax credit* is progressively withdrawn in line with increases in earnings or savings.

Means-tested benefits See *Means test*.

Means testing See *Means test*.

Normative This term refers to theories or to general writings which set out to argue what should be, rather than just to analyse or explain what is observed.

Panel studies See *Longitudinal studies*.

Paradigm A closely related set of idea or theories that achieve a dominant position within social science and provide a model or blueprint for others.

Pathology In medicine a pathological condition is one which threatens the health of the body. By analogy, some commentators use the term *social pathology* to refer to behaviours or outcomes which they believe are unhealthy for the society or community in which they occur.

Prescriptive See *Normative*.

Social democracy This term was customarily used to refer to political parties that pursued socialist objectives through parliamentary means. The distinction was made between *social democrats*, who believed that capitalism could be reformed by democratically elected governments, and Marxists, who sought revolutionary change through class struggle. In recent years, however, these terms have been used more broadly to refer to parties of the centre left and their supporters.

Social democrats See *Social democracy.*

Social pathology See *Pathology.*

Social structure The pattern of social arrangements within a society or social group. There is no agreement among social scientists as to what are the most important elements of the social structure. Some commentators and theorists point to social divisions based upon class, gender, ethnicity, sexuality or disability, some to economic and political institutions, some to the family and local communities of place, ethnicity or faith. In general a structural account or explanation is one which emphasizes the ways in which human behaviour is shaped and constrained by social structures, as opposed to explanations that emphasize the importance of *agency.*

Supreme Court (US) The highest court in the judiciary of the USA. It is headed by the Chief Justice and has eight other members, or Justices. All are appointed for life by the President with the consent of the Senate.

Targeted This term is used in two ways in the literature on welfare. First, it refers to benefits and services provided for low-income households, in which usage it is another word for *means test.* Second, it refers to benefits and services provided for those who live in particular localities or are members of designated groups, such as lone parents or people with disabilities.

Tax credit See *Means test.*

Third way This term is variously used as a description, an accolade and a form of abuse. It refers to the broad reappraisal of electoral strategy, philosophy and policy that was undertaken by parties on the centre left in the USA, UK and parts of Europe in the 1990s.

Transmitted deprivation See *Cycles of deprivation.*

Underclass This term is commonly used to refer to groups clearly differentiated from the rest of society by a combination of their poverty and their lifestyle. The extent to which such an underclass exists and, if it does, what has brought it into being is the subject of intense controversy in the USA and Europe.

Universal(ism) In discussions of welfare this term is used to refer to benefits and services that are not subject to a *means test.* This does not mean, however, that they are necessarily available to everyone. They may be paid only to people who have themselves paid contributions in the past, who fall into particular categories or who fulfil conditions regarding their availability for work or level of disability.

War on Poverty The expansion in the USA of welfare, job creation, training and education programmes that was authorized by the Economic Opportunity Act of 1964.

Workfare This term refers to the requirement that welfare claimants must fulfil specific work requirements in return for receiving benefits. Commentators differ, however, over how stringent such requirements have to be for a programme or scheme to be called workfare. Some would include a requirement that claimants participate in educational or training programmes, or even simply attend an interview. Others, however, would restrict the term to pro-grammes that demand that claimaints work for a designated number of hours a week.

Zeitgeist The 'spirit of the age', or the assumptions, beliefs and attitudes that are dominant in a particular period.

Bibliography

Alcock, P. (1996) *Social Policy in Britain*. London: Macmillan.

Alcock, P., Glennerster, H., Oakley, A. and Sinfield, A. (eds) (2001) *Welfare and Wellbeing: Titmuss's Contribution to Social Policy*. Bristol: Policy Press.

Askonas, P. and Frowen, S. (1997) *Welfare and Values: Challenging the Culture of Unconcern*. London: Macmillan.

Bane, M. J. and Ellwood, D. (1994) *Welfare Realities*. Cambridge, MA: Harvard University Press.

Besharov, D. J. and Germanis, P. (2001) Welfare reform: four years later, in D. J. Besharov *et al*. (eds) *Ending Dependency: Lessons from Welfare Reform in the USA*. London: Civitas.

Blair, T. (1995) The rights we enjoy reflect the duties we owe, *The Spectator* Lecture 22 March.

Blair, T. (1996) Speech to CPU Conference, Cape Town, 14 October.

Blair, T. (1997) The 21st century welfare state, Speech to Social Policy and Economic Performance Conference, Amsterdam, 24 January.

Blair, T. (1998a) *The Third Way. New Politics for the New Century*. London: Fabian Society.

Blair, T. (1998b) Building a modern welfare state, Speech in Dudley, West Midlands, 15 January.

Blair, T. (1999) Beveridge revisited: a welfare state for the 21st century, in R. Walker (ed.) *Ending Child Poverty*. Bristol: Policy Press.

Blair, T. (2001) The strong society – rights, responsibilities and reform, Speech in Newport, Shropshire, 30 May.

Borrie Commission (1994) *Social Justice: Strategies for National Renewal*. London: Vintage.

Brown, G. (1999) Equality – then and now, in D. Leonard (ed.) *Crosland and New Labour*. London: Fabian Society.

Brown, M. and Madge, N. (1982) *Despite the Welfare State*. London: Heinemann.

Brundson, E., Dean, H. and Woods, R. (eds) (1998) *Social Policy Review 10*. London: Social Policy Association.

Bryner, G. (1998) *Politics and Public Morality*. London: Norton.

Bull, D. (2000) Foreword, in R. Link and A. Bibus, *When Children Pay: US Welfare Reform and Its Implications for UK Policy*. London: Child Poverty Action Group.

CBPP (1999) Low unemployment, rising wages fuel poverty decline (www.cbpp. org/9-30-99pov.htm).

CDF (1999) Extreme poverty rises by more than 400,000 in one year (www.childrendefense.org/release990822.html).

Danziger, S. and Gottschalk, P. (1985) Are we losing ground? *Focus*, 8(3): 1–12.

Deacon, A. (ed.) (1996) *Stakeholder Welfare*. London: Institute of Economic Affairs.

Deacon, A. (ed.) (1997) *From Welfare to Work: Lessons from America*. London: Institute of Economic Affairs.

Deacon, A. (1998) The Green Paper on welfare reform: a case for enlightened self interest? *Political Quarterly*, 69(3): 306–11.

Deacon, A. (1999) Dependency and inequality: a false polarity in the poverty debate? *Journal of Social Policy*, 28(1): 166–73.

Deacon, A. (2000) Learning from the USA? The influence of American ideas on New Labour thinking on welfare reform, *Policy and Politics*, 28(1): 5–18.

Deacon, A. (2001) Introduction: the realities of welfare reform, in D. J. Besharov *et al.* (eds) *Ending Dependency: Lessons from Welfare Reform in the USA*. London: Civitas.

Deacon, A. and Mann, K. (1999) Agency, modernity and social policy, *Journal of Social Policy*, 28(3): 413–35.

Dean, H. and Woods, R. (eds) (1999) *Social Policy Review 11*. London: Social Policy Association.

De Parle, J. (1994) Daring research or social science pornography? *New York Times*, 9 October.

Department for Education and Employment (2000) *Jobs for All*. London: HMSO.

Department for Education and Employment (2001) *Towards Full Employment*, Cm 5084. London: HMSO.

Department of Social Security (1998a) *A New Contract for Welfare*, Cm 3805. London: HMSO.

Department of Social Security (1998b) *Beating Fraud is Everyone's Business*, Cm 4012. London: HMSO.

Department of Social Security (1999a) *Opportunity for All*, Cm 4445. London: HMSO.

Department of Social Security (1999b) *Safeguarding Social Security*, Cm 4276. London: HMSO.

Department of Social Security (2000) *The Changing Welfare State*. London: HMSO.

Dolwitz, D. (1997) *Learning from America*. Lewis: Falmer Press.

Donnison, D. V. (1979) Social policy since Titmuss, *Journal of Social Policy*, 8(2): 145–56.

Donnison, D. (1991) *A Radical Agenda*. London: Rivers Oram Press.

Donnison, D. (2000) The academic contribution to social reform. *Social Policy and Administration*, 34(1): 26–43.

Drake, M., O'Brien, M. and Biebuyck, T. (1982) *Single and Homeless*. London: HMSO.

Driver, S. and Martell, L. (1998) *New Labour: Politics after Thatcherism*. Cambridge: Polity Press.

Driver, S. and Martell, L. (2000) Left, right and the third way, *Policy and Politics*, 28(2): 147–61.

Duerr Berrick, J. (1998) Targeting social welfare benefits in the United States: policy opportunities and pitfalls, Paper presented to Conference of the International Social Security Association, Jerusalem, January.

Duncan, S. and Edwards, R. (1997) Lone mothers, paid work and the underclass debate, *Critical Social Policy*, 17(4): 29–49.

Duncan, S. and Edwards, R. (1999) *Lone Mothers, Paid Work and Gendered Moral Rationalities*. London: Macmillan.

Dwyer, P. (1998) Conditional citizens? Welfare rights and responsibilities in the late 1990s, *Critical Social Policy*, 18(4): 493–517.

Dwyer, P. (2000) *Welfare Rights and Responsibilities: Contesting Social Citizenship*. Bristol: Policy Press.

Dwyer, P. and Heron, E. (1999) 'Doing the right thing'. Labour and welfare reform: a new moral order? *Social Policy and Administration*, 33(1): 91–104.

Edelman, P. (1997) The worst thing Bill Clinton has done, *Atlantic Monthly*, March: 43–55.

Ellwood, D. (1988) *Poor Support*. New York: Basic Books.

Ellwood, D. (1996) Welfare reform as I knew it: When bad things happen to good policies, *American Prospect*, 26: 22–9.

Ellwood, D. and Summers, L. (1986) Is welfare really the problem? *Public Interest*, 83: 57–78.

Etzioni, A. (1995) *The Spirit of Community*. London: Fontana Books.

Etzioni, A. (1997) *The New Golden Rule*. London: Profile Books.

Etzioni, A. (1998) Introduction, in A. Etzioni (ed.) *The Essential Communitarian Reader*. Oxford: Rowan and Littlefield.

Etzioni, A. (2000) *The Third Way to a Good Society*. London: Demos.

Field, F. (1981) *Inequality in Britain: Freedom, Welfare and the State*. London: Fontana Books.

Field, F. (1995) *Making Welfare Work*. London: Institute of Community Studies.

Field, F. (1996) A rejoinder, in A. Deacon (ed.) *Stakeholder Welfare*. London: Institute of Economic Affairs.

Field, F. (1997) *Reforming Welfare*. London: Social Market Foundation.

Field, F. (1998) *Reflections on Welfare Reform*. London: Social Market Foundation.

Field, F. and Piachaud, D. (1971) The poverty trap, *New Statesman*, 3 December.

Fimister, G. (ed.) (2001) *An End in Sight?* London: Child Poverty Action Group.

Gentry, P., Johnson, C. and Lawrence, C. (1999) Moving in many directions: state policies, pregnancy prevention and welfare reform, Paper presented to the 21st Research Conference of the Association for Public Policy Analysis and Management Washington DC, 6 November.

Giddens, A. (1998) *The Third Way: The Renewal of Social Democracy*. Cambridge: Polity Press.

Giddens, A. (2000) *The Third Way and Its Critics*. Cambridge: Polity Press.

Glennerster, H. (2000a) *US Poverty Studies and Poverty Measurement: The Past Twenty-five Years*, CASE paper 42. London: London School of Economics.

Glennerster, H. (2000b) *British Social Policy Since 1945*. Oxford: Blackwell.

Goodman, A., Johnson, P. and Webb, S. (1997) *Inequality in the UK*. Oxford: Oxford University Press.

Gowing, M. (1975) Richard Morris Titmuss 1907–1973, *Proceedings of the British Academy*, 61: 401–28.

Grant, L. (2000) Crossing the Atlantic: US welfare reform and the degradation of poor women, in H. Dean, R. Woods and R. Sykes (eds) *Social Policy Review 12*. London: Social Policy Association.

Greenstein, R. (1985) Losing faith in 'Losing Ground', *New Republic*, 25 March: 12–17.

Hall, P. (1976) *Reforming the Welfare*. London: Heinemann.

Harrington, M. (1997) *The Other America*, rev. edn. New York: Touchstone Books.

Hills, J. (1998) *Income and Wealth: The Latest Evidence*. York: Joseph Rowntree Foundation.

HM Treasury (1998) *The Working Families Tax Credit and Work Incentives: The Modernisation of Britain's Tax and Benefit System No. 3*. London: HMSO.

HM Treasury (1999) *Tackling Poverty and Extending Opportunity: The Modernisation of Britain's Tax and Benefit System No. 4*. London: HMSO.

HM Treasury (2000) *Tackling Poverty and Making Work Pay – Tax Credits for the 21st Century: The Modernisation of Britain's Tax and Benefit System No. 6*. London: HMSO.

Hogget, P. (2001) Agency, rationality and social policy, *Journal of Social Policy*, 30(1): 37–56.

House of Commons Employment Committee (1996) *Second Report: The Right to Work/Workfare*. London: House of Commons Session 1995–6 HC 82.

Jencks, C. (1997) The hidden paradox of welfare reform, *American Prospect*, 32: 33–40.

Jencks, C. and Edin, K. (1990) The real welfare problem, *American Prospect*, 1: 31–50.

Jenkins, S. (1999) Income dynamics, in J. Hills (ed.) *Persistent Poverty and Lifetime Inequality: The Evidence*. HM Treasury Occasional Paper 10. London: HMSO.

Joffe, C. (1998) Welfare reform and reproductive politics on a collision course, in C. Lo and M. Schwartz (ed.) *Social Policy and the Conservative Agenda*. Oxford: Blackwell.

Joseph, K. (1972) The cycle of deprivation, Speech to Conference of Pre-School Playgroups Association, 29 June.

Joseph, K. (1974) Britain: a decadent new Utopia, Speech in Birmingham, 19 October, reprinted in *Guardian*, 21 October.

Kaus, M. (1986) The work ethic state, *New Republic*, 7 July: 22–33.

Kaus, M. (1992) *The End of Equality*. New York: Basic Books.

King, D. (1995) *Actively Seeking Work: The Politics of Unemployment and Welfare Policy in the United States and Great Britain*. Chicago: University of Chicago Press.

King, D. and Wickham-Jones, M. (1999) Bridging the Atlantic: the Democratic (Party) origins of welfare to work, in M. Powell (ed.) *New Labour New Welfare State?* Bristol: Policy Press.

Kleiman, M. (1997) Coerced abstinence: a neopaternalist drug policy initiative, in L. Mead (ed.) *The New Paternalism*. Washington, DC: Brookings Institution Press.

Klein, R. and Rafferty, A. (1999) Rorschach politics: Tony Blair and the third way, *American Prospect*, 45 (July/August): 35–43.

Lane, C. (1985) The Manhattan project, *New Republic*, 25 March: 14–15.

Layard, R. and Phillpot, J. (1991) *Stopping Unemployment*. London: Employment Policy Institute.

Lee, P. and Raban, C. (1988) *Welfare Theory and Social Policy*. London: Sage.

Leisering, L. and Walker, R. (eds) (1998) *The Dynamics of Modern Society*. Bristol: Policy Press.

Lerman, R. (1999) Retreat or reform? New US strategies for dealing with poverty, in H. Dean and R. Woods (eds) *Social Policy Review 11*. London: Social Policy Association.

Levitas, R. (1998) *The Inclusive Society?* London: Macmillan.

Lewis, G., Gewirtz, S. and Clarke, J. (eds) (2000) *Rethinking Social Policy*. London: Sage.

Lister, R. (ed.) (1996) *Charles Murray and the Underclass Debate*. London: Institute of Economic Affairs.

Lister, R. (1997) *Citizenship: Feminist Perspectives*. London: Macmillan.

Lister, R. (1998) From equality to social exclusion: New Labour and the welfare state, *Critical Social Policy*, 18(2): 215–25.

Lister, R. (1999) Reforming welfare around the work ethic, *Policy and Politics*, 27(2): 233–46.

Lodemal, I. and Trickey, H. (eds) (2001) *An Offer You Can't Refuse: Workfare in International Perspective*. Bristol: Policy Press.

Lowe, R. (1999) *The Welfare State in Britain Since 1945*, 2nd edn. London: Macmillan.

McCarthy, M. (1986) *Campaigning for the Poor: CPAG and the Politics of Welfare*. London: Croom Helm.

Macnicol, J. (1987) In pursuit of the underclass, *Journal of Social Policy*, 16(3): 293–318.

Macnicol, J. (1999) From 'problem family' to 'underclass', 1945–1955, in R. Lowe and H. Fawcett (eds) *Welfare Policy in Britain: The Road from 1945*. London: Macmillan.

Madge, N. (ed.) (1983) *Families at Risk*. London: Heinemann.

Magnet, M. (1993) *The Dream and the Nightmare*. New York: William Morrow.

Main, T. (1997) Homeless men in New York City: toward paternalism through privatization, in L. Mead (ed.) *The New Paternalism*. Washington, DC: Brookings Institution Press.

Mandelson, P. (1997) *Labour's Next Steps: Tackling Social Exclusion*. London: Fabian Society.

Mann, K. (1986) The making of a claiming class – the neglect of agency in analyses of the welfare state, *Critical Social Policy*, 15: 62–74.

Mann, K. (1992) *The Making of an English Underclass?* Buckingham: Open University Press.

Mann, K. (1994) Watching the defectives: observers of the underclass in the USA, Britain and Australia, *Critical Social Policy*, 41: 79–99.

Marquand, D. (1996) Moralists and hedonists, in D. Marquand and A. Seldon (eds) *The Ideas that Shaped Post-war Britain*. London: Fontana.

Marquand, D. and Seldon, A. (eds) (1996) *The Ideas that Shaped Post-war Britain*. London: Fontana.

Marshall, T. H. (1973) Richard Titmuss: an appreciation, *British Journal of Sociology*, 24(2): 137–9.

May, M., Brundson, E. and Craig, G. (eds) (1997) *Social Policy Review 9*. London: Social Policy Association.

Maynard, R. (1997) Paternalism, teenage pregnancy prevention and teenage pregnancy services, in L. Mead (ed.) *The New Paternalism*. Washington, DC: Brookings Institution Press.

Mead, L. (1978) Federal social policy: the need for citizenship, Unpublished memorandum, 13 December.

Mead, L. (1986) *Beyond Entitlement*. New York: Free Press.

Mead, L. (1987) The obligation to work and the availability of jobs: a dialogue, *Focus*, 10(2): 11–19.

Mead, L. (1988a) The hidden jobs debate, *Public Interest*, 91: 40–58.

Mead, L. (1988b) Why Murray prevailed, *Academic Questions*, 1(2): 23–31.

Mead, L. (1991) The new politics of the new poverty, *Public Interest*, 103: 3–20.

Mead, L. (1992) *The New Politics of Poverty*. New York: Basic Books.

Mead, L. (1997a) Citizenship and social policy: T. H. Marshall and poverty, *Social Philosophy and Policy*, 14(2): 197–230.

Mead, L. (1997b) Welfare employment, in L. Mead (ed.) *The New Paternalism*. Washington, DC: Brookings Institution Press.

Mead, L. (1997c) The rise of paternalism, in L. Mead (ed.) *The New Paternalism*. Washington, DC: Brookings Institution Press.

Mead, L. (1997d) From welfare to work, in A. Deacon (ed.) *From Welfare to Work: Lessons from America*. London: Institute of Economic Affairs.

Millar, J. (2000) *Keeping Track of Welfare Reform: The New Deal Programmes*. York: Joseph Rowntree Foundation.

Miller, S. M. (1987) The legacy of Richard Titmuss, in R. Titmuss *The Philosophy of Welfare*. London: Allen & Unwin.

Milne, S. (1994) 'Everybody's talking about . . . Communitarianism, *Guardian*, 7 October.

Mincy, R. and Pouncy, H. (1997) Paternalism, child support enforcement and fragile families, in L. Mead (ed.) *The New Paternalism*. Washington, DC: Brookings Institution Press.

Moynihan, D. P. (1997) *Miles to Go*. Cambridge, MA: Harvard University Press.

Murray, C. (1982) The two wars against poverty, *Public Interest*, 69: 3–16.

Murray, C. (1984) *Losing Ground*. New York: Basic Books.

Murray, C. (1986a) No, welfare isn't really the problem, *Public Interest*, 84: 3–11.

Murray, C. (1986b) It's not fair to the children, *New Republic*, 6 October, 22.

Murray, C. (1987) In search of the working poor, *Public Interest*, 89: 3–19.

Murray, C. (1988) *In Pursuit of Happiness and Good Government*. New York: Touchstone Books.

Murray, C. (1993) The coming white underclass, *Wall St Journal*, 29 October.

Murray, C. (1996) Rejoinder, in R. Lister (ed.) *Charles Murray and the Underclass*. London: Institute of Economic Affairs.

Murray, C. (1998) Charles Murray, in R. Nye (ed.) *The Future of Welfare*. London: Social Market Foundation.

Murray, C. (2001) *The Underclass Plus Ten*. London: Civitas.

Novak, M. (ed.) (1987) *The New Consensus on Family and Welfare*. Washington, DC: American Enterprise Institute.

Novak, M. (1998) *Is There a Third Way?* London: Institute of Economic Affairs.

Nye, R. (1998) Foreword, in F. Field, *Reflections on Welfare Reform*. London: Social Market Foundation.

Oakley, A. (1991) Eugenics, social medicine and the career of Richard Titmuss, *British Journal of Sociology*, 42(2): 165–94.

Oakley, A. (1997) *Man and Wife*. London: Flamingo.

Oakley, A. and Ashton, J. (eds) (1997) *The Gift Relationship Revisited*. London: Penguin.

Orloff, A. (1998) Ending the entitlement of poor mothers, expanding the claims of poor employed parents, *European Forum on Recasting the Welfare State Working Paper*. Florence: European University Institute.

Orloff, A. (2000) Ending the entitlement of poor mothers: changing social policies, women's employment and caregiving in the contemporary United States, in N. Hirschman and U. Liebert (eds) *Women and Welfare: Theory and Practice in the US and Europe*. New York: Rutgers University Press.

Page, R. (1996) *Altruism and the British Welfare State*. Aldershot: Avebury.

Page, R. (2000) For richer, for poorer? New Labour and the welfare state, *Social Policy and Administration*, 34(5): 614–19.

Pantazis, C. and Gordon, D. (2000) *Tackling Inequalities: Where Are We Now and What Can Be Done?* Bristol: Policy Press.

Phillips, M. (1997a) Workfare for lone mothers: a solution to the wrong problem?, in A. Deacon (ed.) *From Welfare to Work: Lessons from America*. London: Institute of Economic Affairs.

Phillips, M. (1997b) *The Sex Change State*. London: Social Market Foundation.

Piachaud, D. and Sutherland, H. (2001) Child poverty and the New Labour government, *Journal of Social Policy*, 30(1): 95–118.

Pinker, R. (1977) Preface, in D. Reisman, *Richard Titmuss: Welfare and Society*. London: Heinemann.

Piven, F. F. (1996) Was welfare reform worthwhile? *American Prospect*, 27 (July/August).

Plant, R. (1996) Social democracy, in D. Marquand and A. Seldon (eds) *The Ideas that Shaped Post-war Britain*. London: Fontana.

Powell, M. (ed.) (1999) *New Labour, New Welfare State?* Bristol: Policy Press.

Preston, R. H. (1979) *Religion and the Persistence of Capitalism*. London: SCM Press.

Price, D. (2000) *Office of Hope*. London: Policy Studies Institute.

Rainwater, L. and Yancey, W. (1967) *The Moynihan Report and the Politics of Controversy*. Cambridge, MA: MIT Press.

Reisman, D. (1977) *Richard Titmuss: Welfare and Society*. London: Heinemann.

Reisman, D. (1982) *State and Welfare*. London: Macmillan.

Responsive Communitarian Platform (1998) Rights and responsibilities, in A. Etzioni (ed.) *The Essential Communitarian Reader*. Oxford: Rowan and Littlefield.

Rivlin, A. (1973) Forensic social science, *Harvard Educational Review*, 43: 61–75.

Robinson, S. J. (1987) R. H. Tawney's theory of equality. PhD thesis, University of Edinburgh.

Rose, H. (1981) Rereading Titmuss: the sexual division of welfare, *Journal of Social Policy*, 10(4): 477–502.

Rowlingson, K., Whyley, C. and Warren, T. (1999) *Wealth in Britain: A Lifecycle Perspective*. York: Joseph Rowntree Foundation.

Rutter, M. and Madge, N. (1976) *Cycles of Disadvantage*. London: Heinemann.

Ryan, W. (1967) Savage discovery: the Moynihan report, in L. Rainwater and W. Yancey (eds) *The Moynihan Report and the Politics of Controversy*. Cambridge, MA: MIT Press.

Ryan, W. (1976) *Blaming the Victim*. New York: Vintage Books.

Sacks, J. (1997) *The Politics of Hope*. London: Jonathan Cape.

Schoor, A. (1984) Comment, *Journal of Social Policy*, 13(4): 401–3.

Seldon, A. (1996) Ideas are not enough, in D. Marquand and A. Seldon (eds) *The Ideas that Shaped Post-war Britain*. London: Fontana.

Selznick, P. (1992) *The Moral Commonwealth*. Los Angeles: University of California Press.

Selznick, P. (1998a) Foundations of communitarian liberalism, in A. Etzioni (ed.) *The Essential Communitarian Reader*. Oxford: Rowan and Littlefield.

Selznick, P. (1998b) Social justice: a communitarian perspective, in A. Etzioni (ed.) *The Essential Communitarian Reader*. Oxford: Rowan and Littlefield.

Shaw, M., Dorling, D., Gordon, D. and Davey Smith, G. (1999) *The Widening Gap: Health Inequalities and Policy in Britain*. Bristol: Policy Press.

Sheehy, G. (2000) *Hillary's Choice*, rev edn. New York: Ballantine Books.

Sinfield, A. (1978) Analyses in the social division of welfare, *Journal of Social Policy*, 7(2): 129–56.

Skocpol, T. (1996) Bury it, *New Republic*, 12 August: 20–1.

Skocpol, T. (2000) *The Missing Middle*. New York: Norton.

Spragens, T. (1998) The limits of Libertarianism, in A. Etzioni (ed.) *The Essential Communitarian Reader*. Oxford: Rowan and Littlefield.

Starobin, P. (1998) The daddy state, *National Journal*, 28 March: 1–4.

Stacey, J. (1998) The right family values, in C. Yo and M. Schwartz (eds) *Social Policy and the Conservative Agenda*. London: Macmillan.

Supplementary Benefits Commission (1980) *Annual Report 1979*. London: HMSO.

Taylor-Gooby, P. (1981) The empiricist tradition in social administration, *Critical Social Policy*, 2: 6–21.

Teles, S. (1996) *Whose Welfare? AFDC and Elite Politics*. Kansas City: University Press of Kansas.

Timmins, N. (1996) *The Five Giants: A Biography of the Welfare State*. London: Fontana.

Titmuss, R. M. (1938) *Poverty and Population*. London: Macmillan.

Titmuss, R. M. (1942) *Parents Revolt*. London: Secker and Warburg.

Titmuss, R. M. (1950) *Problems of Social Policy*. London: HMSO.

Titmuss, R. M. (1958a) The social division of welfare, in *Essays on the Welfare State*. London: Unwin University Books.

Titmuss, R. M. (1958b) Social administration in a changing society, in *Essays on the Welfare State*. London: Unwin University Books.

Titmuss, R. M. (1968) *Commitment to Welfare*. London: Unwin University Books.

Titmuss, R. M. (1970) *The Gift Relationship*. London: George Allen & Unwin.

Titmuss, R. M. (1974) *Social Policy*. London: George Allen & Unwin.

Titmuss, R. M. (1987) *The Philosophy of Welfare*. London: Allen & Unwin.

Titterton, M. (1992) Managing threats to welfare: the search for a new paradigm of welfare, *Journal of Social Policy*, 21(1): 1–23.

Townsend, P. (1973) *The Social Minority*. London: Allen Lane.

Townsend, P. (1975) *Sociology and Social Policy*. London: Allen Lane.

Townsend, P. (1979) *Poverty in the United Kingdom*. London: Allen Lane.

Townsend, P., Davidson, N. and Whitehead, M. (1988) *Inequalities in Health*. London: Penguin Books.

Vaizey, J. (1983) *In Breach of Promise*. London: Weidenfeld and Nicholson.

Viet-Wilson, J. (2000) States of welfare: a conceptual challenge, *Social Policy and Administration*, 34(1): 1–25.

Walker, A. (1996) Blaming the victims, in R. Lister (ed.) *Charles Murray and the Underclass*. London: Institute of Economic Affairs.

Walker, R. (1991) *Thinking about Workfare: Evidence from the USA*. London: HMSO.

Walker, R. (1998a) The Americanisation of British welfare: a case-study of policy transfer, *Focus*, 19(3): 32–40.

Walker, R. (1998b) Unpicking poverty, in C. Oppenheim (ed.) *An Inclusive Society: Strategies for Tackling Poverty*. London: Institute for Public Policy Research.

Walker, R. (ed.) (1999) *Ending Child Poverty*. Bristol: Policy Press.

Weaver, K. (1998) Ending welfare as we know it, in M. Weir (ed.) *The Social Divide: Political Parties and the Future of Activist Government*. Washington, DC: Brookings Institute.

Weaver, K. (2000) *Ending Welfare as We Know It*. Washington, DC: Brookings Institute.

Welshman, J. (1999) Evacuation, hygiene, and social policy: the *Our Towns* report of 1943, *Historical Journal*, 42(3): 781–807.

Welshman, J. (n.d.) Pathology, politics and professionalisation: Richard Titmuss and creation of social services departments, 1960–70, Unpublished paper.

White, S. (1998) Interpreting the Third Way: not one road but many, *Renewal*, 6(2): 17–30.

Wilkinson, R. G. (1989) Class mortality differentials, income distribution and trends in poverty 1921–1981, *Journal of Social Policy*, 18: 307–35.

Wilkinson, R. G. (1996) *Unhealthy Societies: The Afflictions of Inequality*. London: Routledge.

Willets, D. (1996) *Blair's Gurus*. London: Centre for Policy Studies.

Willets, D. (2000) *Browned-off: What's Wrong with Gordon Brown's Social Policy?* London: Politeia.

Williams, F. (1989) *Social Policy: A Critical Introduction, Issues of Race, Gender and Class*. Cambridge: Polity Press.

Williams, F. (1999) Good-enough principles for welfare, *Journal of Social Policy*, 28(4): 667–87.

Williams, F. (2000) Travels with nanny. Destination good enough. A personal/intellectual journey through the welfare state, Inaugural lecture, University of Leeds, 11 May (www.leeds.ac.uk/CAVA).

Williams, F., Popay, J. and Oakey, A. (1999) *Welfare Research: A Critical Review*. London: UCL Press.

Wilson, J. Q. (1985) The rediscovery of character, *Public Interest*, 81: 3–17.

Wilson, J. Q. (1993) *The Moral Sense*. New York: Free Press Paperbacks.

Wilson, J. Q. (1995) *On Character*. Washington, DC: The AEI Press.

Wilson, J. Q. (1997) Paternalism, democracy and bureaucracy, in L. Mead (ed.) *The New Paternalism*. Washington, DC: Brookings Institution Press.

Wilson, W. J. (1987) *The Truly Disadvantaged*. Chicago: Chicago University Press.

Wilson, W. J. (1997) *When Work Disappears*. New York: Alfred Knopf.

Wiseman, M. (1999) In the midst of reform: Wisconsin in 1997, *Focus*, 20(3): 15–22.

Wiseman, M. (2001) Making work for welfare in the United States, in I. Lodemel and H. Trickey (eds) *An Offer You Can't Refuse: Workfare in International Perspective*. Bristol: Policy Press.

Index

RISK, SOCIAL POLICY AND WELFARE

Hazel Kemshall

- What is the relevance of the concept of risk to social policy?
- Has risk replaced need as the key organizing principle of welfare provision?
- Do current trends support the contention that policy development is risk-based?

Traditionally, need has been the major mechanism for allocating resources in public services, and social policy texts have addressed various state responses to social problems and the alleviation of need. However, in a period of state retrenchment and welfare restriction, rationing and targeting have become more intense. This book explores the extent to which, as a result, risk and vulnerability have replaced need as the key principles of welfare rationing and provision. It begins with an introductory overview of current theories on risk and goes on to examine the relevance of risk to social policy and welfare developments. This is achieved by drawing on recent social policy and case examples from health, the personal social services and mental health. Written with the needs of undergraduates in mind, the author presents clear examples, provides summaries of key points and makes suggestions for further reading throughout. The result is a highly accessible introduction to the concept of risk for students, researchers and professionals in social policy, health and social welfare.

Contents
Introduction: risk, responsibility and social policy – Risk in contemporary society – Key organizing principles of social welfare: from need to risk – Health care: the rise of risk, health promotion and rationing – Child protection and the care of the elderly: need, vulnerability and risk – Mental health, mental disorder, risk and public protection – The new risk-based welfare – Glossary – Bibliography.

176pp   0 335 20409 0 (Paperback)   0 335 20410 4 (Hardback)

COMPARATIVE SOCIAL POLICY
THEORY AND RESEARCH

Patricia Kennett

- What are the social policy processes and outcomes across different societies?
- How are these shaped by social and economic conditions?
- What are the limitations and potential of cross-national research?

Comparative Social Policy explores the new context of social policy and considers how cross-national theory and research can respond to the challenges facing welfare. These challenges include changing demographic trends and economic conditions which have been accompanied by the emergence of new needs and risks within and across societies. This book extends and deepens cross-national research by exploring the theoretical and conceptual frameworks through which social policy and welfare systems have been understood. It critically examines different policy processes and welfare outcomes, as well as the ethnocentrism and cultural imperialism which has permeated cross-national epistemology and methodology. The author concludes by reflecting on how cross-national research can illuminate the complex and diverse processes leading to discrimination and inequality across borders. This leads to a consideration of how it can contribute to the implementation of welfare provision appropriate to the social and economic conditions of contemporary societies. *Comparative Social Policy* is an essential text for undergraduate and masters level students of social policy, and an invaluable reference for researchers embarking on cross-national social research.

Contents
Introduction – Globalization, supranationalism and social policy – Defining and constructing the research process – Theory and analysis in cross-national social policy research – Development, social welfare and cross-national analysis – Ethnicity, gender and the boundaries of citizenship – Australia, Britain and Japan – The future of comparative social policy research – Notes – Glossary – Bibliography.

192pp   0 335 20123 7 (Paperback)   0 335 20124 5 (Hardback)

EDUCATION IN A POST-WELFARE SOCIETY

Sally Tomlinson

'This book provides a context for understanding educational policies which is currently missing from education and social policy courses. It should be compulsory reading.'

Len Barton, University of Sheffield

- What have been the positive and negative effects of education reforms in recent years?
- Why are the moderate successes of state education unrecognised and education portrayed as 'failing' or in crisis?
- How has the reproduction of privilege by education persisted despite a rhetoric of equality and inclusion?

Education in a Post-welfare Society provides a concise and critical overview of education policy, as government in Britain has moved from creating a welfare state to promoting a post-welfare society dominated by private enterprise and competitive markets. Concentrating particularly on the past twenty years, Sally Tomlinson places in context the avalanche of legislation and documentation that has re-formed education into a competitive enterprise in which young people 'learn to compete'. She also demonstrates how a relatively decentralised education system became a system in which funding, teaching and curriculum were centrally controlled, and education narrowed to an economic function. Chronologies of education acts, reports and initiatives are provided at the beginning of the first six chapters. Major legislation is summarised, and an extensive bibliography and annotated suggestions for further reading provide additional guidance. The result is an invaluable resource for students of social policy and education; as well as educational researchers and professionals.

Contents
Introduction – Social democratic consensus? Education 1945–79 – Market forces gather: education 1980–7 – Creating competition: education 1988–94 – The consequences of competition: education 1994–7 – New Labour and education: 1997–2000 – Centralizing lifelong learning – Education and the middle classes – Equity issues: race and gender – Education and the economy – Conclusion: Education in a post-welfare society – References – Index.

224pp   0 335 20288 8 (Paperback)   0 335 20289 6 (Hardback)